PRAISE FOR

PRAISE FOR

THE UGLY UNDERNEATH

"Absolutely incredible! I laughed, I cried, and I could not put it down. Carlos invites readers into a world few dare to talk about, yet he does so with such honesty and warmth that you connect with him both as a father and a son and a leader. This book is a powerful reminder of how often we box up our emotions—and how healing begins when we learn to unpack them."

—REBECCA BENDER, survivor, leader, and founder of Elevate Academy

"Carlos's vulnerability in sharing the realities of this work is powerful. Too often, those of us in helping professions carry these experiences silently. *The Ugly Underneath* breaks that silence, reminding us there is nothing wrong with being impacted by the work; it means we care. His stories give both grace and preparation for those walking into this space. This book is a gift to the profession."

—MELISSA KAISER, international expert consultant on human trafficking and vicarious trauma

"*The Ugly Underneath* is raw, brave, and profoundly human. Carlos Rodriguez writes with the kind of honesty that only comes from walking through both darkness and grace. His story shines a light on the unseen toll of protecting children—and the quiet redemption that comes when compassion refuses to quit. As someone who shares this calling, I see in Carlos a fellow warrior of light whose courage reminds us that love, when lived out, is the truest form of faith."

—JESSICA R. MUÑOZ, MSN, APRN-RX, FNP-BC, founder of Ho'ōla Nā Pua and Pearl Haven

"Carlos offers a rare and deeply personal insight into the career of a Washington State Police officer, detailing his journey from a non-commissioned officer trainee to a specialist investigator in the harrowing field of internet sexual crimes against children.

His candid accounts reveal the profound personal impact of exposure to child sexual abuse material (CSAM) and the challenges of investigating these unimaginable crimes. While some of his graphic descriptions may be difficult to read, especially for those unfamiliar with such investigations, this book provides a fascinating and eye-opening read.

The personal toll of this work is poignantly captured, making it a compelling read for anyone interested in the realities of law enforcement and child protection."

—**DR. JOE SULLIVAN**, director of Forensic Solutions

THE UGLY UNDERNEATH

NAVIGATING THE EMOTIONAL TOLL OF INVESTIGATING CRIMES AGAINST CHILDREN

CARLOS RODRIGUEZ

RIVER GROVE BOOKS

Published by River Grove Books
Austin, TX
www.rivergrovebooks.com

Distributed by River Grove Books

Design and composition by Greenleaf Book Group
Cover design by Greenleaf Book Group
Cover images used under license from ©Unsplash.com

Publisher's Cataloging-in-Publication data is available.

Print ISBN: 979-8-90052-000-1

eBook ISBN: 979-8-90052-001-8

First Edition

This book is dedicated to:

*Vitamin K, my first real love. We didn't always
get it right, but we didn't get it all wrong. Thanks
for loving me when I didn't always deserve it.*

*My Boo Boo, the man in the moon is still smiling.
You keep me grounded. To my son, I always knew it
was you and not an apple. I love you both so much.*

*To my parents for showing me the
best way you knew how.*

*To my MECTF family for not letting me fail.
"For the children."*

"We will walk through hell to get the devil."

—MECTF detective

CONTENTS

INTRODUCTION

"I could never do what you do."

I hear those words a lot, even now that I am retired from investigating crimes against children. At first, I would say, "Thank you." Well, because that's the polite thing to do. When other law enforcement officers would tell me those words I would say, "Thanks, someone has to do it."

I must admit, when it came from law enforcement, after a while it made me angry. Angry because it shouldn't be a choice to protect a kid or go after someone who wants to do evil things to a child. I know now that wasn't fair for me to get angry. Not everyone is cut out to work these types of crimes, just like not everyone is suited to play a professional sport, build a rocket, or conduct open heart surgery. I did the work because I could.

People asked me how I coped with the violence and pain that adults inflict on kids. How did I keep it together when face-to-face with a man or woman who used a child for their own sick sexual pleasure?

Well, as long as I can remember, I put things in mental boxes to process conflict or deal with the uncomfortable things. As with anything, there are pros and cons with how I store these boxes.

This book is my way to unpack some of my boxes by sharing them with you. These boxes contain stories and events that I experienced growing up before I worked crimes against children or was even a police officer. These stories put me on a path to help others.

These experiences helped me cope with my work. These stories are important because they ultimately prepared me to work the cases I did. The boxes are filled with successes, but more importantly they contain mistakes I made, mistakes you can avoid.

For my fellow law enforcement family: I challenge you to take the time to process how this work impacts you and those around you. It's necessary to, if you want to stay healthy while working in this space.

For those of you that are not law enforcement, this book will give you a better understanding of what it's like to work these cases and have some insight into what those who investigate these horrible acts endure.

In 1993 I was fortunate to become a part of the Washington State Patrol (WSP). I was employed by WSP for twenty-seven years, for twenty-five of which I was a law enforcement officer, a state trooper. I spent most of my career conducting investigations, but I didn't start to investigate crimes against children until May of 2012. The best way to explain my career is I got to do some pretty cool shit. I loved it.

I attribute my success to busting my ass and being in the right place at the right time. It also helped that I looked like a kid. Ages ago I thought it was a curse, but now? It's not so bad.

I remember going to see the movie *Soldier* with Kurt Russell and Jason Scott Lee, and the box office attendant asked me, "Can I see your ID?"

I said, "Are you serious?"

"Yes, it's rated R."

I was twenty-six years old at the time and had been a trooper for two years. My youthful appearance was a blessing, though. I think it kept me alive. It allowed me to work undercover investigating auto-theft rings and mid- to upper-level drug trafficking organizations (DTOs). When people found out I was a cop and not an auto thief or a "thug," they were always shocked.

The most rewarding part of my career was investigating crimes against children. It was also the most difficult. I worked in that capacity for nearly eight years. Like I said, I loved my job, but it came at a cost.

Investigating crimes against children is a lot to take on. It can suck the life out of a person. You start to compartmentalize things so you can do the work. For me I became detached from my own emotions.

I had a hard time saying no when people asked for help. For me it wasn't an option. The answer was always yes.

The subject matter itself: overwhelming. The case load: overwhelming. The number of cases compared to the number of resources to do the work was and still is disproportionate.

Then there was the pressure I put on myself to succeed. The necessity to be successful and help others. The thoughts in the back of my mind, the self-doubt.

Can I really help this person? Will I find this kid? That weighed on me a lot. Some of it still does. The ones I didn't find. The ones I failed to help.

If you are out there doing this work, whether you believe it or not, it affects you. You won't know how much until you aren't doing the work any longer. If you don't take care of yourself, this work will tear you down slowly. It will affect your family, the people around you, and ultimately it will negatively impact your ability to complete your mission.

When I worked these cases, I didn't realize how much they affected me. I was selfless in my pursuit to help others, but in doing so I negatively impacted other areas of my life. It affected me then, and still does today.

I wasn't the best father, husband, partner, or friend. I wasn't horrible, but there are things I know I could have done better. The activities I chose to do to cope with my work took away from my time with friends and family. My ability to turn off my emotions didn't come with directions. I lacked the ability to turn off emotions individually. It was like switching off different circuit breakers and then finally flipping off the master breaker switch. Thing is, when I turned the master breaker back on, some of the switches failed to activate.

My life decisions resulted in my divorce, which wasn't the greatest experience for my kids.

I am no hero. The things I share regarding my work are from my perspective, but I did not accomplish anything I set out to do alone. It was always a team effort. All my successes are because others shared the same goal and wanted to do good things.

The topics in this book are painful to digest, and it is difficult to comprehend why someone would do such horrific things to children. If you find yourself having a difficult time reading this book, please stop reading and take a break. This book will still be here when you are ready to pick it back up. Some of the names in this book have been changed. This includes some detectives that are still doing the work. All the names of victims and survivors have been changed out of respect and to protect their privacy.

Even though some names have been changed, these events are real. This is my story and how I remember these events happening. I hope you learn from some of my mistakes and successes.

ONE

DAVID

1

In 1992, I worked at a retail store called Mervyn's. Mervyn's was like a JCPenney but with no catalog. My first job there was scrubbing toilets and waxing the tiled floors. After four days of that, management moved me to receiving. I unloaded merchandise from trailers. Every day was the same: Truck drops off trailer. Open said trailer to reveal a sea of brown cardboard boxes. Move said boxes from said trailer onto our dock. Unpack the boxes.

About a year later I transferred to the children's department. I was nineteen years old and selling OshKosh B'gosh to moms. It wasn't exciting, but it was a job.

My time in the children's department was limited. The store created a new position called area coordinator of customer service. I had no idea what the responsibilities were, but it meant no more little overalls. More importantly it was a 75-cent raise and considered a promotion.

On top of that I learned we were getting new store management, so I decided to wear a tie to work every day. I figured the new managers would see me dressed up and think I was more important than I really was. You know, look the part, get the part.

It worked.

A few months later I was helping in the jewelry department during a big sale. A little boy wanted to buy his mom a necklace. The little guy must have been six, maybe seven years old. He pressed his plump face on the glass case and pointed. "That one."

I said, "This one?"

"Mm-hmm."

"That is a great choice, sir!"

His aunt smiled as she watched us. She happened to be the head of the WSP's Human Resources Division. She liked how I treated her nephew and suggested I apply for the WSP. I was hired the following year.

My first assignment was at the WSP headquarters (HQ) in Olympia, Washington, as a noncommissioned office trainee stuffing envelopes and filing paperwork. Noncommissioned means I was not a law enforcement officer. I was a civilian employee of the WSP. The WSP employs many people that are noncommissioned. Without them the WSP would not be able to function.

HQ was in the General Administration building on the State Capitol Campus. The four-story building was a modern architectural wonder when it was built in 1954, but not in 1993 when I started there. The walls looked like an old man with stress cracks for wrinkles. I remember the air vents used to spit out little black specks. Two men in light blue jumpsuits ran tests on the air and told us it was fine. One guy who worked in the office thought we were all going to die from it.

When I told people I worked for the WSP, most asked if I was a cop. Most people automatically assume that when a person works for a police agency they are a cop or a dispatcher. I wasn't either, and

I had zero desire to become a state trooper. I enjoyed organizing paperwork by day and attending community college at night.

Eventually I became the mail boy for the agency sorting and delivering mail. We didn't have the internet or email yet. I was a real-life Norville Barnes, the mail clerk in the Coen Brothers film *The Hudsucker Proxy*, but without the "Hoopla" and I'm no schmo.

2

Two years later on Mother's Day I woke up to screams: "NO! NO! NO!"

It was my girlfriend, Julie. I met Julie on a blind date set up by one of my buddies from high school. I had stayed the night and was sleeping on her living room floor. She was in her mother's bedroom at the back of the house. I could hear Charlotte, Julie's mom, talking to her, but I couldn't make out what they were saying.

When I saw Julie, tears were rolling down her face. "David was in a car crash. We need to go to the hospital."

David was Julie's oldest brother. I had only met David a few times. I remembered playing video games with him at a family Christmas party. We didn't talk much except about the video game. He was married and his wife, Beth, was pregnant with my future nephew Eli. Most of the time at the party he spent sitting with Beth. He sat next to her the way someone wants to be next to someone they love. That's the best way to describe it.

I eventually heard the story. Earlier that morning, David and his father-in-law, Sam, had gone fishing. They were driving home on State Route 512 and thought their canoe, which was strapped to the top of their little truck, was coming loose. David had pulled onto the shoulder so they could check the canoe.

State Route 512 consists of two lanes in each direction lined with fir trees and thick yellow brush called Scotch broom. David and Sam both exited the truck.

Sam said, "I'm good on this side. How about you?"

David said, "All good here."

Those were the last words Sam heard David say.

A drunk driver drifted onto the shoulder and struck them both. David was standing on the driver's side, closest to the "slow lane," and was hit first. The canoe came loose and swallowed Sam, who was on the passenger's side. The force of the other vehicle pushed the truck over Sam, but the canoe shielded him, saving Sam's life.

3

We rushed to the hospital. Other family members were already there. Beth, David's wife, was there.

I watched as Julie's family learned David did not survive. In that moment I thought, *He won't meet his boy. His kid won't know his dad.*

I remember taking a few steps back to give them space. I was new to their family, and I didn't know everyone. I looked on as they cried. They embraced each other, attempting to comfort one another. I didn't know what to do.

Eventually I went home and left Julie with her family. Later that night the local news reported on the collision. I can still see David's single white sneaker lying in the road surrounded by broken glass and pieces of plastic.

Why did they show that? What purpose did that serve? I lay down in my bed, pulled my blanket over my head, and cried silently until I fell asleep.

4

The next day I drove to work, but I don't remember the drive. I remember sitting at my desk. The hum from the fluorescent lights was louder than usual. I stared at the empty wall behind my computer.

I picked up a pen and began to write a letter to the chief of the state patrol. I don't know why I thought he would read it, but I just felt it was what I should do. In the letter I detailed what had happened to David and how it made me feel. I told the chief I was going to be a state trooper. I was going to prevent others from the pain Julie's family was going through. When I finished writing, I folded the letter so it would fit into a white legal-sized envelope, wrote "CHIEF" on the front, and sealed it.

After sorting the mail, I picked up the letter, added it to my mail cart, and, fixing a smile on my face, pushed the metal cart down the hall toward the chief's office. The cart's little black wheels squeaked, announcing I was on my way.

The chief's administrative assistant smiled at me as I entered the room.

"Good morning, Faith."

"Good morning, Carlos!"

I put the mail into a wooden box on her desk with my letter to the chief at the bottom of the mail stack. Then I turned around and left.

About thirty minutes later I heard a knock on one of the mail room walls. Roger Bruett was the chief of the WSP then. Tall with strong features and neatly dressed, he resembled Disney's Mr. Incredible but with dark hair. My interactions with him previous to this had been limited, but all positive. I had never seen him in the mail room. I stood up quickly.

He said, "Carlos, are you okay?"

I thought, *Shit. Chief knows my name.*

"Yes, sir."

"You should go home."

"No, sir. I have work to do. I am okay." I was not okay.

He paused. "We will be okay here. You should go home."

I felt so numb. I rubbed my hands and then my arms as if I was cold. When I realized the chief was noticing what I was doing, I quickly dropped my arms down to my sides. I said, "I have a lot to do here, sir."

His lips pressed tightly together. He said nothing. Then he raised his arms like a conductor slowing the tempo of an orchestra and said, "This . . . will all be here when you come back." He moved a few steps closer to me. "If not for you, then for them. They need you right now."

"I . . . don't know what to do, sir." I told myself to breathe. "I mean it. What I wrote. This shouldn't happen. It's not right."

"You can still do that, but not today. Today, they need you. Buy them groceries. Run errands. Just be there."

The chief was right. I thanked him and went home. I ended up taking the rest of the week off and did whatever Julie's family needed.

5

"State trooper? You mean the guys that pull you over? The cops with the funny hat and bowties?"

That was the response from most when they found out what I was testing for. Most thought I was crazy. They never said it, but I could see it on their faces. The disbelief. The doubt. I had a lot stacked against me, but what they thought was irrelevant. I was going to be a state trooper.

State troopers historically were over six feet tall because there used to be a height requirement. When I applied, this was no longer a rule because of a little thing called discrimination. Even so, most people still thought troopers had to be at least six feet tall.

I am not six feet tall. I am five foot six. I barely weighed 135 pounds. On top of that, I looked like a young teenager.

Was I strong? Not physically.

Expert marksman? No. I had never shot a real gun.

Did I drive fast? Well, my driving record at the time said yes.

It didn't matter. This was going to happen.

6

July 5, 1995, was my first day at the WSP Academy. It wasn't easy for me. I wasn't the worst cadet, but I wasn't the best either. Cadets, that's what we were called, trooper cadets.

When I first arrived at the academy I checked in at the front office. They sent me to a classroom where I waited with my new classmates for directions. From there we were released in groups to the multipurpose building to pick up our PT gear.

The instructors had us stand at attention while we waited for them to tell us what to do next. Several cadets showed up with facial hair. This was not appreciated by the instructors, and they began to bark at the cadets. Before I could focus on what they were saying, I heard, "OH! MY! GOD!"

It sounded like Gunnery Sergeant Hartman from *Full Metal Jacket*.

He continued yelling, "What am I looking at! Did the WSP lower the age limit!?"

Another trooper said, "Not that I know of, Trooper Matthews."

Shit. They were talking about me. And double shit. It was Trooper

Al Matthews. I had never met him, but I knew who he was. You see, his wife worked in the WSP budget and fiscal office. When I worked in the mail room, I delivered mail to her most days. Before I left for the academy, she told me, "I told Al how excited you are for the academy. He is so funny. He told me, 'We will see how excited he is once he gets here.'"

Before that I was given the advice to blend in and try not to attract too much attention. A trooper had told me, "Be a chameleon; that way they don't yell at you as much."

I realized that was not going to happen.

Trooper Matthews was our TAC officer, which is similar to a drill sergeant. The other trooper stood directly in front of me. He was much taller than me. I stared straight ahead and focused on his chest. Trooper Matthews stood to my right. I could feel the brim of his campaign hat against the side of my head.

"What is your name, cadet?"

"Cadet Rodriguez, sir!"

"Are you old enough to drive, cadet?!"

The heat of his words hit my face like when you open an oven. "Yes, sir!"

"How old are you? Seventeen?! Did we hire a teenager? Are you a teenager?"

"No, sir!"

"Cadet! What are you going to do when you pull over a six-foot-five trucker and he is drunk!"

"I will arrest him, sir!"

"You will? You are going to arrest him?"

"Yes, sir!"

"Well, you will have your chance to prove that to me."

After the instructors finished yelling at us, we were directed to a classroom. I remember a different academy instructor writing out all the ranks in the WSP on a large whiteboard in front of the class. He was one of the six-foot-plus troopers. He started with the chief at the top and made his way down through the ranks. He stopped at trooper.

Below the word "TROOPER" he drew a toilet. This toilet had a long pipe that trailed down into a square box. Inside of the box he drew what he described as all the shit that went down the toilet. Underneath the shit he wrote "trooper cadet."

He turned around and looked at us. He tapped the whiteboard next to the box with his middle finger and said, "That's you. You are below the shit."

He circled the words "trooper cadet" and then drew an arrow up to the word "TROOPER."

He said, "It's my job to get you up here."

I thought, *I hate this place.*

7

That night I lay in my bed and thought, *This is a mistake.*

Man, I wanted to quit. What was I thinking? I was crazy; this was just crazy.

Then I remembered why I was there. I thought of David and then I thought of Julie. I closed my eyes. I could see David's single white sneaker sitting in the roadway, surrounded by pieces of auto glass. I fell asleep.

The next morning, there were several empty chairs in our classroom. The academy sergeant told us some cadets had decided to quit. He told us being a state trooper was not for everyone. I felt some relief. I wasn't alone. Other people had thought this was a mistake too.

Sitting there in the classroom I asked myself, *Who am I?*

I answered, *I am a Washington state trooper.*

As the days went on, more empty chairs appeared and so did my self-doubt. Each time it showed up, I asked myself, *Who am I?*

Each time the answer was the same. *I am a Washington state trooper.*

I worked hard to keep my chair full. On January 23, 1996, I graduated from the 78th Trooper Basic class and was sworn in as a Washington state trooper.

TWO

LISA

1

On October 11, 1981, I was nine years old, and we lived in Colorado Springs, Colorado, in a rambler-style house with a finished basement. I opened the rear sliding glass door to my house and ran past my mom. She yelled something at me, but I didn't listen. I was a brat. My mom used to tell me, "One day when you have your own kids, you will know how difficult you were to raise."

She was right. Luckily for me my kids are much better than I ever was. I continued downstairs.

I liked that house, but it was built on a flood plain, so it flooded twice. I remember my parents being upset, but I liked when it happened. To me it meant I got new stuff. I remember staring down at the carpet in the basement through several inches of flood water. The shag carpet swayed back and forth like the seaweed in the opening scene of the movie *Jaws*. I remember wondering if there were any baby fish in there. Of course there weren't, but I was a kid and didn't know any better.

My room was downstairs just past my grandma Lisa's room. I had my own room with a set of bunk beds. I slammed my door closed so hard, my poster of *The Fall Guy*'s Heather Thomas ripped free from the door. Instead of taping it back up, I threw the poster on the bottom bunk. I reached into my Pac-Man running shorts and pulled out a small horny toad.

Horny toads were everywhere in my neighborhood. They are called horny toads because they have little spikes all over their backs. They are not really toads, though; they are lizards—bad-ass mini dinosaurs that can squirt blood out of their eyes as a defense tactic. Every now and then I would put one in my underwear drawer for a few days.

I admit it is gross keeping a lizard in my underwear drawer, but at the time I thought it was cool. One time my mom was putting some of my laundry away and one of the little guys scared the shit out of her, resulting in me getting in trouble.

I liked to scare my mom. I scared her whenever I got the chance. She had this weird, delayed scream. If I jumped out at her, she would stare at me for a few seconds. This was followed by her screaming at the top of her lungs while maintaining her stare. Like *Invasion of the Body Snatchers*—Donald Sutherland *Body Snatchers*, not the one with Nicole Kidman. It was creepy. Even though me scaring her resulted in her scaring me back, it was worth it.

2

I threw the new horny toad in my dresser and ran back upstairs. I was in a hurry because today Grandma Lisa was teaching me how to play checkers.

I was nine, and she was fifty-six. I stopped at the bottom of the stairs, posing in my best running stance, and then raced up the stairs as fast as I could. Once at the top of the stairs I launched off the last stair and landed with both feet together.

My grandma said, "Mijo!"

She wasn't mad. I could do no wrong in her eyes. She was waiting for me at our simple, dark brown wood dining room table with six wooden chairs. No cushions. We didn't keep anything on the table. I don't think we ever ate at it either. We usually ate downstairs using metal TV trays. At least that's how I remember it.

Grandma Lisa was my dad's mom. Her voice was scratchy, I think because she smoked cigarettes. Her hair was dyed dark red, and when she hugged me, she smelled like Avon perfume with a pinch of ashtray. She called me her king and she treated me like one.

The checkerboard was already set up on the table. She explained the rules and what "king me" meant, and then she let me pick what color I wanted. I picked black every time. After a few hours of checkers she said, "Mi rey, I'm going to watch *Tom Jones*."

Every Sunday she watched the *Tom Jones Show* followed by *All in the Family*, or "The Archie Bunker Show" as she called it.

I said, "Grandma, I like *CHiPs* better."

She said, "Erik Estrada? Pendejo! He thinks he is hot shit."

I don't know why she didn't like him, and I didn't care. Ponch was my favorite. Everybody knew John sucked.

Grandma Lisa's room was small. If you stood outside of her room and looked in, you could see her small sleeper sofa and a little table placed next to the sofa to your left. On the little table was a thin-framed picture of Jesus Christ, a candle, and an ashtray. It was White Jesus. You know, the one with blue eyes.

Once you walked into her room and sat on the sofa you would find her RCA television sitting on the floor against the wall across from the sofa. The TV tube was surrounded by brown wood and had two large dials on the front—one for the channels and the other for the volume.

I didn't like to sit on her sofa or sleep in her room. Sometimes she asked me to sleep with her. I always said yes, but after about twenty minutes I opened my eyes and saw White Jesus. White Jesus scared me. I mean, what was he looking at? Once Grandma fell asleep, I snuck away and left her with White Jesus.

3

I ran into her room and plopped on the floor. Sometimes I got bored when I was in her room and did stupid stuff. One time I got on all fours and dragged my forehead on the carpet in circles. I remember humming the theme song to *Raiders of the Lost Ark* by John Williams while I did it.

After about ten minutes my forehead started to sting. I sat up and searched for the sting with my fingers. It felt wet. I ran to the bathroom to look in the mirror. The friction from the carpet and my skin had created a shiny pink circle in the center of my forehead. It eventually turned into a brown scabby reminder that I was a dummy. Like I said, stupid stuff.

Tom Jones was over, and Grandma told me, "Mi rey, go get your dad. Archie Bunker is next."

I ran upstairs, yelling for my dad. By the time the show started, my dad was on the sofa. He was wearing a white plain tee, faded blue jeans, and white socks. My dad was extremely fit, but his T-shirts were always too tight. My little sister, Carmen, was snuggled next to Dad.

4

My grandma Lisa was not nice to my sister. I have no idea why. It was little things like making her wait just a little bit longer than me or yelling at her for singing even if I was singing at the top of my lungs. She didn't treat us the same. I remember it made me uncomfortable.

Carmen was the best little kid. Her hair was dark brown and usually pulled back into one big, braided ponytail. Her hair was so long it went past her waistline. Sometimes my mom would do Carmen's hair like Pippi Longstocking, but my sister didn't like it—not the way it looked, but the process. It looked like my mom was harvesting hair as she raked my sister's head with a brush. Sometimes I thought Carmen's head was gonna pop off as the brush ripped her head back. When she put the brush down, it was full of hair that had used to be on my sister's head.

Carmen didn't complain about anything for the most part. I remember she laughed at all my jokes. Even the bad ones. She still does.

"Carmen, what did the skunk say to the tree?"

She put her hand on her chin, tapping her tiny index finger over her lips. "Umm . . ."

I never waited for her to answer. I just blurted out the punch line. "You better leaf, cuz I stink."

Carmen threw her head back and started laughing. She covered her mouth with both of her tiny hands, trying to keep the giggles from spilling out. When she stopped laughing, she always did this thing where she would shake her head side to side like she couldn't believe how great my joke was.

I said, "Do you get it? The tree can't leave cuz it doesn't have legs!"

She said, "That's a good one."

Thinking back now, I didn't understand my own joke.

5

My mom was upstairs somewhere when the show started. I don't remember her ever watching with us. Grandma was lying down on the floor next to me. Our feet were toward the TV, our heads closer to her sofa. The theme music started. She wrapped her arm around me, pulling me into her. She gave the best hugs. She released her grip and then grabbed me again, as if she was carrying me and had to adjust so she wouldn't drop me.

This hug was different. This hug didn't feel good; it hurt. I shrugged her off me. "Grandma!"

She released me all the way this time. I turned to face her. Grandma was lying on her back, eyes closed, mouth wide open. She inhaled quickly. It sounded like a pig squealing.

"Cut it out, Grandma," I said, smiling. She was always trying to make us laugh.

The squeals turned into loud snorts, like snoring, but hurried like she couldn't breathe. The snorts became louder. There was no set rhythm or pattern to the sounds.

My heart raced. "It's not funny."

Her body tightened, toes pointed straight, arms pressed against her sides. She relaxed, tightened, relaxed. It hurt to watch. She was in pain. Her arms flopped around. My dad was off the sofa and kneeling next to her.

"Son, get your mom. Tell her to come down here. Take your sister with you."

Yellow oatmeal rolled out of Grandma's mouth. It smelled like when I vomited a little in my mouth and it burned my nose.

"Go! Run!"

I ran upstairs searching for my mom, my sister right behind me. I could hear my dad pleading with Grandma, "Mom! Mom!" He called for my mom. "Gracie! Gracie!"

The next thing I remember is being posted at the front window of our house looking into our cul-de-sac for the ambulance. Why was it taking so long to get to us?

Sirens. I could hear sirens. I saw red lights reflecting off the neighbor's houses. They were almost to my house. Then the lights and sirens faded away.

I felt cold all over. "They missed us." The sirens sounded like they were getting closer. "They are coming. I see them!"

They faded again. I thought, *They can't find us.*

I threw open the front door and ran outside to catch them. They passed the cul-de-sac a third time. I was in the middle of the cul-de-sac waving my arms in the air yelling at them. "Here! Over here!"

Some neighbors watched me from their porch, and others peered from their windows. I was in a full sprint and lost my footing. As soon as I hit the ground I pushed back up and away from the asphalt. I brushed a few pebbles off my cheek, checking my knees and then my palms. *Yup, that's blood.*

I ran toward where I had last seen the ambulance.

Brake lights.

The ambulance backed up to me. I pointed to my house. "That one, it's that one, downstairs."

6

The next day the pain from the asphalt had spread to the rest of my body. My head hurt. I was in my room lying on my bottom bunk trying to make sense of everything. Then I heard a man sobbing and realized it was my dad. I felt panicked; I had never heard him cry before. I jetted out of my room and ran up the stairs faster than I had ever run before. My chest was pounding. When I finally reached the top of the stairs I was confused. My dad wasn't there.

Instead, I found my mom standing alone in the living room holding her own hands in front of her. She must have heard me running up the stairs because she was looking at me. She gave me the type of smile a stranger gives when they don't want to smile back but feel obligated to.

Mom told me to sit down on the couch. She wasn't crying, but the edges of her nostrils were red, and an empty Kleenex box on the coffee table told me she had been. She placed one hand on my shoulder and said, "Wait here while I get your sister."

"Okay, Mom."

Mom came back with Carmen. My sister climbed up onto the couch next to me. She rested her head on my arm, leaning into me like she had with my dad the night before. I put my arm around her. She felt hot. Stuff like that bugs me. Kind of like how a pair of socks with a bad seam irritates your big toe. Not this time, though; I needed her next to me.

Mom said, "Grandma is gone."

Her words hit me like an object. The weight of it, you know, it was something that I could feel. This was real.

She started to say more, but I interrupted her. I said, "Do you mean she is dead?"

I don't remember her answer.

There are things that happen to us in life that don't make any sense. This was one of those things for me. It still lives within me. I learned later Grandma died from a blood clot. As I grew older,

I learned what that meant, but it didn't change how it hit me at the time.

This was my first time packing.

This was my first box.

THREE

TRIPLE A WITH A BADGE

"How many tires did you change today, troop?"

Cops like to flip each other shit, but it's all in good fun. My first assignment as a trooper was in downtown Seattle. The Seattle city cops called us "Triple A with a badge" because we frequently assisted disabled motorists. Funny thing is the first time I ever changed a tire was at the WSP Academy. We actually had a course on changing tires.

When I first learned I was assigned to the Seattle freeway, I was mortified. It was called the Concrete Jungle or the Slab. It wasn't the largest beat, but it was the busiest in the state. Older troops told me that working a year in Seattle was like working three years in another beat.

To my surprise, I loved working the Slab. Every day was an adventure with something new to do or solve. I didn't want to work anywhere else. Not everyone liked it, though, and the turnover of troopers was high. That meant I quickly became a senior trooper for that area.

My goal was to arrest one hundred DUIs a year for my entire career. Man, back then I was so naive. It's funny how I thought I would stay on the freeway my entire career. I mean, troopers do it, but that wasn't the path I was destined for.

I worked the road for about four years. When you see the state troopers on the side of the freeway or investigating collisions, that is called "working the road" or "the road." After those four years I became an auto-theft detective who drove a little black Honda hatchback.

Shortly after that I was promoted to sergeant. I never had the desire to be promoted any higher than that. Being a sergeant allowed me to lead people as well as continue to do the work. I liked that.

The WSP is a large agency. This allowed me to be a part of some amazing teams and create some great memories. As a sergeant I managed a statewide program and multiagency task forces. I was lucky enough to lead state and federal law enforcement officers and agents.

When I was a kid my dad would tell me, "Son, work hard at everything. If you do that, people will want to be a part of what you are doing, or they will want you to help them."

He asked me once, "You know what they call a guy that doesn't work?" My dad never waited for me to answer, so I just waited for him to tell me. "They don't." Then he would laugh and nudge me with his elbow. "You get it? It's because the guy doesn't work! Seriously, son, if they don't like to work, they are losers."

I listened to my dad, and I worked my ass off. That translated to being asked to put in for specialty positions and to lead teams. I'll admit, sometimes I didn't know what I was doing or at least it felt that way. Especially if it was something I had never done before.

Not knowing made me anxious, but it didn't stop me from trying new things. I told myself if someone else could do it, then so could I. Then I just did it. I made myself do it. It doesn't mean that I executed everything perfectly, but I learned from my mistakes, and it all worked out.

It's important to challenge yourself. If you don't, you will always be stuck in the same spot.

I think life is scary sometimes, but if it wasn't scary, then it would be boring, and to me boring isn't living.

MECTF

1

"Hey Carlos, how are you?"

It was Randy Drake or RTBB, which stands for Randy the Big Boss. I don't remember exactly where I was when he called me, but it was in 2011. I was a sergeant and supervising a detachment of troopers in Bremerton, Washington.

I first met RTBB in 2006 when he was promoted to lieutenant. He was looking for someone to take care of his team, the West Sound Narcotics Enforcement Team, or WestNET, and someone recommended me for the job. His team focused on mid- to upper-level DTOs, which are usually affiliated with or operated by gangs.

At the time, I managed the Drug Evaluation and Classification Program (DECP) for Washington state, which is responsible for training law enforcement to detect whether a person is or is not under the influence of a certain category of drug.

I agreed to meet with Randy the following week after I finished presenting to the WSP command staff at our strategic advancement forum (SAF). Imagine a slow death via PowerPoint slides filled with charts and statistics. That was SAF. After the SAF, Randy and I went to get "coffee."

For those of you that are not law enforcement, getting coffee means you are going to sit down and talk about things. Yes, coffee was a part of it, but not a requirement. I know because I do not drink coffee. I like the smell of it but not the taste. When I was a young trooper, a senior trooper told me, "See how long that lasts, Boot." Well, it lasted. I still don't drink coffee.

Randy reminded me of Dale Earnhardt Jr.—his hair, his confidence, and some of his mannerisms. Like Dale, Randy is a winner. The guy succeeds at what he sets his mind to. We sat down. He asked, "Who was the lady you were talking to before SAF?"

I thought, *This guy was surveilling me.* "That's Elaine. She works with me."

"What does she do?"

"Everything. She is the backbone of my program. Without her there is no DECP."

"I get that, but what is she to you?"

He was getting at something, but I couldn't put my finger on it.

"Technically she is my admin assistant, but we are a team."

He said, "The reason I ask is because I have someone special to me at WestNET. She is like your Elaine. I am looking for someone that will look after her. I think that someone might be you."

Randy asked me a few more questions. He asked if I would be interested in spending a day at WestNET to see if investigating mid- to upper-level DTOs was for me. I agreed. Investigating narcotics at this level was all new to me. This would be a challenge, but I wanted to give it a shot. I put in for the position and was selected.

The person he wanted me to take care of likes to be called Chitty. Like *Chitty Chitty Bang Bang*. Her last name is Chittenden, so Chitty makes sense. She is one of a kind.

I did my best to take care of Chitty during my time there, but when it came down to it, she took care of me. She reminded me to eat and when it was time to go home. Even though I didn't always listen to her, she still reminded me. Chitty took care of everyone. That's just what she did.

When I got the position at WestNET, luckily for me RTBB was my direct supervisor. He taught me there is a solution for every problem. Sometimes you just have to search a little harder to find that solution. He used to say, "The hardest part is to get everyone to sit down at the table and look at each other. Step one, let's get everyone to the table."

2

"I'm good, Randy. What's new?"

I was happy to hear from Randy. It was no secret that I wanted to work with him again. I had left WestNET for a short stint managing the governor's protection detail and was then supervising some troopers.

Randy was now the captain at the Washington State Fusion Center (WSFC), a unified counterterrorism "all crimes" fusion center, incorporating agencies with intelligence, critical infrastructure, public safety and preparedness, resiliency, response, and recovery missions. The WSFC's mission is to support the public safety and homeland security missions of state, local, tribal agencies, and private sector entities. Randy had an opening at the center, and I wanted it.

He asked, "Do you want the good or the bad news first?"

I thought, *Shit, I'm not getting this spot.* I said, "Bad."

"Sweeting transferred internally."

I was right. This meant I was not getting the spot. Sweeting was another WSP sergeant. Since I was not in the Investigative Assistance Division (IAD) any longer and Sweeting was, he was able to transfer internally before the position would be advertised outside of the division.

I said, "Well, shit."

Randy then asked, "What do you know about MECTF?" I knew he was talking about the Missing and Exploited Children Task Force.

"Don't they put the posters of missing kids on the semitrucks?"

"No. That's a different unit. I think you would be a good fit there. Do you know Bill Steen?"

"Yeah. I know Bill."

"He is in the task force. Give him a call. He can tell you what they do. It needs work, but you can do a lot of good there."

3

"Bill, people are like doors. That guy is a door that says pull, and you're pushing. You need to change how you talk to him."

Bill was having an issue with someone. There are doors that say push, some say pull, some are revolving, some are open, some closed, and some are locked. Some doors don't even lead anywhere. The trick is figuring out what kind of door you are dealing with. Once you know that, you can get to where you need to go.

I first met Bill Steen when we worked the road as troopers in

Seattle. Bill is a former marine recon guy with a degree in biochemistry. Basically, you can dump him in the middle of nowhere and he can MacGyver some shit to get the job done. When he worked with me on MECTF, he was on SWAT and a sniper.

We all know someone who says they know everything about everything. That's Bill. Except Bill literally does know everything about everything. *Cheers* had Cliff Clavin Jr., and the WSP has Bill Steen.

4

I gave Bill a call. He was excited to have me cross-train with the task force. Bill told me MECTF investigated crimes against children. He told me they were serving a search warrant, and I should go and observe to see if it was for me. I agreed to go.

I observed MECTF and the High-Tech Crimes Unit (HTCU) serve a search warrant at a residential duplex. HTCU is a group of highly skilled detectives that conduct forensic analysis of digital media.

MECTF and HTCU were there to search for evidence of trading and possessing child sexual abuse material (CSAM), commonly known as child porn. I hate that term. Pornography is something that is legal and is widely accepted in society. There is nothing legal or acceptable about children being raped.

Not only do these images and videos document the exploitation and abuse of children, but when these images are shared across the internet, these children suffer re-victimization each time the image of their sexual abuse is viewed. The National Center for Missing and Exploited Children (NCMEC) states "67 percent of [CSAM] survivors said the distribution of their images impacts them differently than the hands-on abuse they suffered because the distribution never ends and the images are 'permanent.'"[1]

CSAM is nothing short of an epidemic. I quickly learned that CSAM was traded using peer-to-peer (P2P) networks. If you remember Napster or LimeWire, they were P2P networks. With Napster, members shared music. With LimeWire, you could trade other files besides music, but it was mostly used to download pirated music.

A P2P network is a decentralized network architecture where all participating computers, known as peers, are equally capable of sharing and receiving resources. In a P2P network, there is no central server or controller, and each peer can act as both a client and a server. Even today there are thousands upon thousands trading CSAM, and law enforcement cannot keep up.

5

During this warrant service a suspect was identified who possessed CSAM. I noticed the task force was not booking the suspect into jail. This made no sense to me. I asked the sergeant in charge why the suspect wasn't being booked.

He explained they did not book suspects if no CSAM was located during a forensic preview. A forensic preview is a search that HTCU conducted looking for CSAM while at the search warrant site. Sometimes HTCU was not able to find CSAM while onsite. Now that didn't mean there was no CSAM; sometimes more advanced software and equipment was required to locate it. In all cases the digital evidence was searched further at the HTCU office using this advanced software and equipment.

---

1   "An Update on Voluntary Detection of CSAM," Tech Coalition, April 11, 2024, https:// technologycoalition.org/resources/update-on-voluntary-detection-of-csam/.

I asked him, "Okay? Why isn't this guy getting booked? We located the images; I think I'm missing something?"

He explained, "Most prosecutors want the full case, and booking the suspect speeds up the timeline to get the case completed."

His answer hurt my brain. This was not an acceptable answer.

If we found a meth dealer with meth during a search warrant, we would book the meth dealer and write a detailed probable cause statement. The full case file would go to the prosecutor's office in a timely manner. If the prosecutor needed the entire case sooner, then we would make it happen. His answer was not correct to my thinking.

In my view it is simple. I like to call it police work. The last time I checked, MECTF and HTCU were still the police. The answer he gave me was an excuse not to work. The technical term is lazy.

When I later became the detective sergeant at MECTF, one of the first changes I made was to book suspects immediately when we located CSAM onsite.

6

I waited a little over a year before I learned I was selected to lead MECTF. The delay wasn't normal for our agency. I was told it was due to state budget cuts and that all vacant positions had been frozen. I found out later that MECTF was being considered for elimination.

When I found that out, I couldn't believe the state would eliminate a task force focused on protecting kids. Crazy, right? I know now MECTF was on the verge of being eliminated. I believe it was for a few reasons. My predecessor wasn't as proactive as I was, and our agency did not provide the task force with the appropriate resources to be successful. I am not saying my agency did not care about these crimes. It absolutely did. The majority of the WSP's resources were not dedicated to combatting crimes against children. After all, the main purpose of the WSP is to enhance public safety and security across Washington state by providing a range of public safety services, including traffic and criminal laws, investigating collisions, assisting motorists, and partnering with other agencies. The focus is mostly on highway safety and criminal law enforcement on our highways and state routes.

Although MECTF was called a task force, we did not have all the resources a task force needs to function.

While at WestNET I had administrative support, six to seven detectives from multiple agencies, grant funding in addition to department funding, and an assigned prosecutor. The community we served knew what our task force did.

MECTF was different, drastically different. Most of my time in MECTF I had two detectives, sometimes only one plus myself. We didn't even have enough personnel to serve a search warrant safely. We had no dedicated administrative support. On top of that, before I joined MECTF, nobody really knew what MECTF did, including me. Under these circumstances, MECTF was destined to fail.

FIVE

"I HAVE TO GO."

1

It was almost the summer of 1989. I was seventeen and we didn't live in Colorado any longer. We had moved to Lawton, Oklahoma, and we were about to move to Ft. Lewis, Washington, which is now known as Joint Base Lewis–McChord or JBLM.

I did not want to move. I was going to be a senior, and although I only had two friends, I didn't want to leave them.

Our house had sold, and we were living in a small apartment. We had a few more weeks until we started our drive to Washington state.

My mom called my sister and me into the living room. Mom was sitting next to my dad on the couch. She was usually working when my dad was home, so having them together at the same time was weird.

Mom looked at both of us and said, "Kids, your dad and I want to talk to you about something."

When my mom talked to us, there was always some sort of lesson. I wasn't in the mood for another lesson right now. They were taking me away from my friends. Then I noticed she was rubbing her hands together as if she was washing them. Something was wrong.

2

Besides selling term life insurance, my mom was a financial advisor. She was and still is an independent woman.

When she moved to the United States, she was fourteen years old and spoke only Spanish. She learned English quickly and won the local spelling bee even with her strong accent. My mother chose not to teach my sister and me Spanish. She feared if we spoke Spanish, we would have an accent and be discriminated against like she was.

"Mijo, it shouldn't matter, but it does. People treat you differently. I don't want that for you or your sister."

Mom taught me a lot of great things, but also some not-so-great things. She would say, "We control our own emotions. Don't let your emotions control you." She started training me early on how to quarantine my feelings.

She also never apologized for anything. Not really. She would tell me, "Carlos, if you are in a disagreement, you say: I'm sorry you feel that way. That way you are not really apologizing, but the other person feels you are."

I remember her being gone most evenings. Carmen and I took care of ourselves until my dad came home.

When my dad was home, he would watch TV. If we interrupted him, he would say, "Shhh! I'm watching a show." I don't think he knew what he was doing or how that affected me. I know now it was his escape and he didn't mean any harm by it.

I did learn from that, though, and years later I sat my kids down and told them, "If I am ever watching a show or a movie and ignore you, I want you to ask me if whatever I am watching is more important than you are. I promise you I will stop and give you my full attention. You two are more important than any show or movie."

I never promised my kids anything unless I was going to honor the promise. My parents made promises they didn't keep. "Tomorrow, we will do it tomorrow." I'm sure the promises were trivial to them, but to me as a kid they were important.

The first time my kids asked me if a show was more important than them, it transported me back to watching my dad on the couch. I just wanted to talk to him. I thought, *Shit. I'm doing it.*

I turned the TV off and gave them my full attention—the attention they deserved and the attention I wanted when I was their age. I'm proud I got that right.

3

My dad loved taking us to Burger King. He used to say, "Don't tell your mom."

Burger King isn't fancy, but to us kids it was the best. Mom didn't like us eating out. At least that's how I remember it. I know now it was because we didn't have much money, and both of my parents worked hard to make sure we had a life better than they did.

Carmen and I always agreed not to tell Mom, but she always found out because, well, we always told Mom.

I can hear my dad ordering at the Burger King front counter, "Three Whoppers, no ketchup, extra pickles."

My dad's logic was simple. He explained it to us every time we went to Burger King. "I always order with no ketchup so they have to make it fresh and not give you one of the premade burgers. You guys can add your own ketchup when we sit down."

My dad ordered us each one full-sized Whopper, hoping we couldn't finish our burgers. This meant more food for him. After a few years Carmen and I began to finish our Whoppers. This meant Dad had to order himself a second one. Even though we always finished our Whopper, he watched us eat with hopeful eyes. As we finished our Whoppers, Dad would get back in line and ordered his second Whopper.

Afterward he would say, "I shouldn't have eaten that last Whopper."

We would say, "Get a Whopper Jr., Dad!"

"Doesn't taste the same. Just does not taste the same."

I know we are talking about him eating two burgers, but the man was super fit. He ran eight to ten miles a day. I wanted to be just like him.

If we didn't eat out, we were stuck eating Hamburger Helper Lasagna, ground beef mixed with canned green beans, or Chef Boyardee mini raviolis.

Today was different, though. This wasn't going to be a conversation about eating out. This was something else.

4

Dad's palms pressed into his thighs like an iron trying to smooth out the wrinkles in his jeans. Only there were no wrinkles to smooth out. He couldn't keep still. My teeth clenched together, scraping side to side. They do that when I get nervous.

I told myself, *You control your emotions. They don't control you.*

Dad was looking out the window. The sun was shining on his face, but he still had dark shadows beneath his eyes. Both of his legs were restless. He blurted out, "Your mom and I are getting a divorce!"

My mom started to scold him, saying this wasn't what they had agreed upon. Their mouths were moving, but I couldn't make sense of any of it. Carmen was eleven years old then and so tiny.

We look a lot alike, my sister and I. Her long hair was gone. I think too many hairbrush sessions with Mom helped her decide to chop it off. We both had wavy hair with Venus flytrap eyelashes. Why can't I remember the look on her face?

I said, "I have to go."

Since the apartment was small, I had to take only a few steps to the front door. I closed it behind me, ignoring my mom as she called my name. She didn't follow me; at least I don't think she did. I got in my gray 1985 Honda Prelude and began to drive.

5

I decided to go to my aunt Lupe's house in Pasadena, California. I cried silently, listening to Judson Spence sing "Forever Me, Forever You" over and over. I love that song.

After about two hours I realized I didn't have enough money to get to my aunt's house, so I turned around and drove home.

6

Turned out my mom was cheating on my dad with a man named Lewis. I remember him being a weak, sickly looking man with glasses, the kind of guy that would back down if you looked at him just right.

My dad suspected she was cheating and one day followed her to a hotel. He confronted my mother and the man. I don't know all that went on in my parents' relationship, but for me as a kid that didn't matter. She wronged him. No, she wronged us. I was so angry.

SIX

RONALD

1

It was November 29, 2009. I was thirty-seven years old, and I still had more pepper than salt in my hair. I was still the supervisor at WestNET. It was Sunday and I was on a day off.

Most Sundays, you can find me practicing paintball with my team. I started playing paintball in the late nineties, which transitioned to competing in tournaments in 2003. I love it because when I play paintball, everything disappears. I have no problems except what is presented to me on the field.

This particular Sunday I was spending the day with my kids, Liv and Noah, instead of playing paintball. We were at a video game store called GameStop. Liv was nine and Noah was six. GameStop had a program where people could trade games. After only one time, my kids were hooked. Today they were seeking out Nintendo DS games.

Liv has analyzed everything as long as I can remember. This included choosing new DS games. If I had let her, she would have spent the entire day studying every game in that store. She held her hands together as if she was praying. "Dad, this feels like a good one." Between her palms was a Kirby Super Star Ultra DS video game case.

"Oh, mm-hmm, yes. I can feel it. It's a good one. I'll hold it for you. See if you can find another good one."

Liv went back to analyzing the games. She stuck her tongue out and pressed it onto her upper lip. She does this when she examines things or is deep in thought. Sometimes her tongue moves slightly back and forth, but it usually remains pressed to her upper lip in the same spot. She still does this even as an adult.

Noah, on the other hand, was in it for the trading. He didn't really play the games. If the box looked cool, he wanted to trade for it. At six he would rather put on a Spider-Man mask and pretend he was fighting Venom or Venom fighting Spidey. He used to get them mixed up all the time.

My cell phone vibrated in my front pocket. "This is Carlos."

"Hey Los, it's Doug."

2

Doug was a trooper that I had worked with a few years back. He left the department to become an FBI agent and was assigned to an office in Northern California. Doug is a tall, lanky, pale-faced red-head. He loves Mike Myers and knows most of the lines from the Austin Powers movies.

Doug sounded serious.

I said, "What's up, man?"

"I'm good, Los. Where are you?"

"I'm at GameStop with the kids trading games."

Doug asked, "Did you hear about the shooting in Lakewood?"

"Yeah. Julie told me about it. She saw it on a Facebook group. I was gonna call Ronnie to ask about it after this."

Ronnie was also a former state trooper and a friend of ours. He had lateraled to the Lakewood Police Department (PD). When an officer laterals from one agency to another, it means that agency acknowledges the officer was a certified law enforcement officer and accepts them as one of their own officers. Oftentimes the officer will complete a shortened training program with the new agency.

When I needed information about what was happening in Lakewood or Pierce County, I called Ronnie. Ronnie was awesome. When he wasn't at work, he would be in some short OP-style shorts or Levi's jeans with a pair of slip-on Vans. No socks. He would say, "You can't wear socks with Vans, man. It's illegal."

Ronnie was always smiling and giving his coworkers shit. If they got mad, he would throw them a shaka sign, and everything was good. We had one troop in our crew from Georgia. Ronnie called him Kentucky. I can still hear the troop saying in his slow Georgia drawl, "I don't see how you can call a boy from Georgia, Kentucky."

3

Doug asked if I knew anything else about the shooting. He was assigned to an FBI task force that investigated gangs.

"Not really. Is it gang related? You coming up here?"

"Yes, I am. It's not for work, though." He stopped talking.

I said, "Okay?"

He said, "It's Ronnie."

"What do you mean it's Ronnie?"

Doug paused again and then said, "Carlos, it's Ronnie. He was one of the officers involved in the shooting."

"What? No, I thought it was Pierce County. Ronnie is Lakewood, man."

"He didn't make it."

"What are you talking about?"

"Ronnie . . . he didn't make it."

Doug's words soaked the sound up from the room. I didn't believe him. I was holding an iced black tea. I took a sip from the straw and tasted mostly melted ice.

"What do you mean? How do you know?"

Liv had stopped studying the games and was focused on me, her tongue still pressed against her lip and with the same intense look on her face.

Doug told me what he knew. As I listened to him, I wanted to fall to the ground, but I continued to stand. He had to be wrong. This couldn't be right. I told him goodbye and ended the call.

"Hey kids, sorry, we gotta go. I need to talk to your mom about something."

I sucked on the straw again, but there was nothing left but ice now. I twirled the cup as if moving the ice around would create more tea. Nothing. I twirled it again then threw it in the trash before leaving the store.

Noah wasn't happy; he was there to trade games. He didn't understand why we were leaving. He dropped his shoulders and stomped his feet in protest as we walked out of the store. He told Liv, "We just got here."

Liv put a hand on each of his shoulders and leaned over to whisper in his ear. Whatever she said calmed him down. We went out to Big Blue, our large fifteen-passenger Chevrolet Express van. Blue only seated twelve people, though. The salesman I bought it from told me it had been retrofitted by the US Navy, and they had used it as a mobile command center. The gray vinyl bench seats were placed so the rear passengers could look at each other, like you were sitting in an old diner booth but with no table in between you. Blue was perfect for road trips and family outings.

I put the kids in the back and then sat in the driver's seat for a while.

My box was full.

My skin turned hot and then went cold. I could feel the condensation form on my nose and forehead. I covered my face with my hands and slowly wiped at the moisture. I broke down. I tried to gather myself before my kids noticed me sobbing. I wonder now if this was what my dad felt like when Grandma died. I could feel their eyes on me.

I heard Noah whisper to his sister, "What's wrong with Dad?"

She said, "He got some bad news and is sad about his friend."

Noah asked, "Is he crying?"

I composed myself and said, "Okay, kids. Are you all buckled up? Click it or ticket!"

I drove us home. As we pulled into our driveway, I asked Liv to watch her brother while I talked to her mom. Julie and I left the kids downstairs and went up to our bedroom. I told her about Ronnie, and she hugged me.

I didn't want to believe it. I didn't believe it. Julie and I watched the news together. I wanted to go to the scene and do something, but that would make it real. I chose to stay home. We left our bedroom and turned on a little TV in our kitchen. The news anchor was announcing the names of four officers. I heard only one name: Ronald Owens.

So strange. I had never heard anybody call him Ronald. I placed my hand on the counter to steady myself. Julie covered her mouth with one hand and squeezed my forearm with the other.

I felt a smaller hand grab my right hand. It was Noah. I hadn't noticed he was standing next to me, watching me. He said, "I'm sorry about your friend Ronald." I kneeled down next to him. He released my hand and wrapped his arms around me. Such a strong hug from such a little boy. He said, "It's okay to be sad."

"Thank you, Bub."

"What happened to Ronald?" His eyes looked so big.

I said, "A bad man killed my friend."

He asked, "Ronald?"

"Yes. Ronald."

We took a break from watching the news. Julie and I sat with the kids at the kitchen table. I told them not to worry about me. I was just sad to not have my friend anymore. We talked about how I did my very best to make sure I came home to them every day and not to worry about me getting hurt. Noah didn't understand.

As we talked, I realized Noah didn't know his dad was a police officer. It made sense. I was in a plainclothes assignment, and the last time I had worn a uniform Noah was only one year old. Noah thought my job was being a "paintball guy," not a police officer.

4

Before this, I made it a point not to talk about what I did around the kids. At least not until they were older. I thought it would keep them from worrying about me.

The first time Noah saw me in a uniform was the day of Ronnie's funeral. I remember him touching one of my gold-plated George

Washington buttons on the cuff of my uniform's sleeve. I squatted down to give him a hug. He hugged me and then grabbed my badge. He said, "Take this off."

I smiled and said, "I have to keep the badge on here, Bub."

"No, the policeman suit."

"Why do you want me to take it off?"

He said, "I don't want you to die."

I was not expecting that. I didn't say anything.

He said, "If you wear this, then bad people will know you are the police. If you don't wear it, they won't try to kill you."

I hugged him again.

He said, "I don't want you to die like Ronald."

I said, "I'm not. I am going to be okay."

He said, "Okay."

I left knowing he didn't believe me. Julie's mom watched the kids while we went to say goodbye to Ronnie.

S E V E N

AGENDAS

1

"Yes. I'm forty-five minutes out. See you soon."

I hung up the phone and pressed my foot down on the accelerator. My black Chrysler 300 felt slower today.

For most of 2010 I managed the Washington state governor's protection detail. My team consisted of eight troopers, and we were responsible for the safety of the governor and her family. The governor's scheduler, Mary, had just advised me some threats had been emailed to her office in reference to the gov. The governor liked us to call her "Gov," so of course we did.

Mary's voice told me the threats disturbed her. Although I lived on the West Coast, I felt like I worked both West and East Coast time zones. Protecting the gov meant keeping up on current events, which did not wait for our time zone. I would rise with the East Coast and rest with the West Coast. My day started with reading the news feeds, social media posts, emails, and the like. Keeping the gov and her family safe meant knowing what to keep them safe from. I felt being well informed helped me to avoid potential embarrassment for my principal.

2

I had learned about this position from one of my friends, Patrick. He ran the protection detail before me, and he had recently been promoted. Patrick was looking for someone to take care of his team and his principal. He asked me if I was interested in the job.

I first met Patrick when we worked the I-5 corridor in downtown Seattle. Patrick is a big personality and has the gift of gab. He was a bartender at a local Irish bar called Kell's before becoming a state trooper.

We don't talk on a daily basis or even hang out, but that doesn't matter. I have a small circle of people that I would not hesitate to respond to if they called and needed help, and they would do the same for me. The last time I spoke with him, he answered, "You good?"

Patrick knew I had never done anything like the protection detail before, but he believed I would succeed. The interview process consisted of not one interview, but three. I made it past the first interview and then had a one-on-one interview with the chief.

3

Chief Bruett was no longer the chief. He had retired before I made it into the academy. The man in charge now was Chief Anderson. When the chief spoke, people listened. To me he appeared to be seven feet tall, but then again everyone looks tall to me. He was a large man but put people at ease when he spoke with them. I learned from him the most important resource any organization has is its people—service with humility. Take care of your people. Provide them with the resources they need. Support them and they will support you and the mission of the agency.

The first time I met the chief was when my brother-in-law David was killed. The next time I saw him I was a new trooper, and he remembered my name.

Every time I saw him, he remembered who I was. He did this with everyone. He valued who I was and what I could do for the citizens of Washington. At least that is how I felt. This is a big reason I stayed with the state patrol. For most of my career the WSP was among the lowest-paid law enforcement agencies in Washington state. It did not matter to me because I enjoyed what I did and who I worked with.

As my interview started, I could see the chief relax as I answered his questions. As he relaxed, I relaxed. This job was important. I was going to be entrusted with protecting his boss. If I fucked this up, it was a fuck-up on multiple levels.

Toward the end of the interview, the chief explained, "As far as the chain of command goes, there is no chain of command. You report to me, and you report to the gov. If there is something you feel I need to know, you tell me." He went on to explain there was no time for delay when it came to getting things done.

It was easy for the chief to say there was no chain of command, but the chain remained. In any other position I had three layers above me. I learned quickly the three layers above me did not like that I reported directly to the chief. I also realized I needed to tread lightly because I might not always be in this position, and someone over me might be my supervisor in the future. Plus, those in the three layers above me had earned those positions and I respected that.

4

After my interview with the chief, I was scheduled to meet with the gov. Before the interview I met Patrick in his office. He handed me a piece of paper and watched as I read it. It was an anonymous email expressing disgust that a candidate being selected to protect the governor had a history of being investigated by our Office of Professional Standards (OPS). OPS is the WSP's internal affairs. The email did not list any names and went on to say that someone with such a long history of problems with the agency should not be considered.

Thing is, I had never been investigated by OPS, so I knew this wasn't about me.

I said, "Okay?"

He said, "Well?"

"What? Do you think this is about me?"

He said, "Well, it isn't about *me*!"

"Patrick, if they didn't want me to get the job, they should have made something up that isn't so easy to disprove."

"Are you sure there isn't anything? She might ask."

"No. Nothing. I mean, I self-reported losing a badge. This isn't me."

A few minutes later we left to meet with the gov. I rolled my shoulders to squeeze some tension out of my body, and we walked into her office. I shook her hand and then sat down across from her and Patrick. They were seated in some fancy soft chairs, and I sat on a sofa across from them. I remember trying to look comfortable. This was difficult because the sofa was deeper than a regular sofa and I'm a "wee fellah."

When I tried to sit on the sofa like a normal-sized person, my feet lifted off the ground. I couldn't sit all the way back or my legs would dangle off the sofa like a toddler. During the entire interview I searched for the right position but never found it.

Every now and then I peeked at Patrick while I answered the gov's questions. He looked nervous, alternating between a forced smile, a half grin, a happy smile, and anxious eyes. He was nervous. His eyes told me, "Don't fuck this up."

The gov asked some basic questions, and the anonymous email never came up. After our talk, the gov's photographer took a photo of the gov and me.

I thought, *Well, if I fucked this up, at least I'll have something to remember it by.*

5

It took me only about thirty minutes to drive to the gov's office, which is located in the legislative building at the state capitol in Olympia, Washington. I guess my car wasn't as slow as it felt. I was wearing a gray two-piece suit, a white shirt, and a navy-and-yellow striped tie. I only wore blue or gray suits. I think brown suits are for attorneys that chase car wrecks, and black suits are for galas or funerals.

I met with Mary, whose desk was in a small foyer in front of the gov's office. She was the keeper of the gate, so to speak. Mary whispered to me that Frank, the chief of staff, was the one to talk to about the threats. Frank's office was located next to the gov's, with an adjoining door connecting them. His office was not as large as the gov's but still a good size. I found him seated at a large wooden table that he used to meet with his staff. Frank got up and shook my hand, then sat back down. I remained standing. He explained he was concerned about some threatening emails about the gov and her family. Part of my job was triaging threats and assessing who had the capacity or resources to carry out their threats. Frank handed me the emails.

> **I hope you have the opportunity to see one of your family members raped and murdered by a sexual predator.**
>
> **You should be burned at the stake like any heretic.**

I told Frank I would take care of it and let him know what I found out within the next few hours. He asked if we should tell the gov.

"No. Let me dig into this and see if the threats hold any weight."

The gov received a lot of threats. Most were from people with opposing views hiding behind a computer screen and never intending to act on their comments. I was not going to bother the gov with this until I knew whether it was valid or not. As I left Frank's office, he waved goodbye. "Thanks, Carlos."

Then I heard, "Yes, thanks, Carlos" coming from a conference speaker on Frank's table. Frank had been on a call and hadn't told me.

I asked, "Who is that?"

Frank told me he was updating the gov's staff. Apparently, multiple people were on the other end. I told him I hadn't realized we were on a call. I said goodbye and continued to walk out of his office.

This was not good. I stopped, turned around, and went back into his office. "One more thing, it will only take a minute." We both stepped away from the table with the speaker. I said to the chief of staff, "Frank, I am going to tell the gov about the threats."

The expression on his face asked, "Why the change?"

"Thing is, the gov is not going to like her staff learning about this before she did."

I left his office and found Mary. I said, "Mary, I need some time with the gov." I did not ask for time off-schedule with the gov unless it was important. When I did it was never good news, and she knew that.

A few moments later Mary said, "Carlos, she is ready for you."

When I entered the gov's office, she was sitting at her desk. The desk was large but looked even bigger because she is a small woman—small in stature, but make no mistake, she was mighty. Her glasses were on the tip of her nose, and she was reading something. She peered over her glasses to see me.

"Carlos. This must not be a happy conversation," she said with a smile on her face while she pushed what she was reading onto the desk.

"Not the best news, Gov." She said nothing and waited for me to continue. "We received some threats. They are ugly. I have them here." I started to read them to her.

She said, "I don't need to hear them."

I said, "At this point the plan is to locate him and go from there. We are in the process of seeing if this is a valid threat or not. The team knows."

She looked perplexed. While this was happening, Frank was standing at an adjoining doorway about fifteen feet away from us.

The gov asked why we were talking about this if I had not vetted the threats yet. I explained how I wanted to notify her since her staff was aware of the threats.

She removed her glasses.

I thought, *Here we go.*

She said, "Why does my staff know about this before me?"

I explained what had happened. She stopped listening and called out, "Mary, please call Frank. I need to speak with him."

Frank was still standing at the doorway between their offices. Mary called his phone. I watched Frank leave the doorway to answer his phone. Mary told us he was on his way.

When Frank showed up, the gov said, "Frank, any threats that come in are handled by my E-poo." E-poo was actually EPU, which stood for the Executive Protection Unit and was the team I managed. "Any threats go to Sergeant Rodriguez and nobody else."

They talked for a while longer. I doubt Frank was pleased with me, but it didn't matter; I had other things to handle. When Frank and I left the gov's office together, Frank remained quiet.

6

I left to meet with the WSP's general detectives about the threats. Although I was in charge of EPU, the general detectives conducted the investigations into threats against the governor. When I got to their office, I learned their administrative assistant was having a hard time identifying the suspect. I knew exactly who to call to find him: Chitty from WestNET. I had depended heavily on her in the past; her spirit was as fiery as her hair was red. She could locate anybody. When she found someone she was searching for, she had a celebration of sorts. She had a little stuffed duck that, when she squeezed it, would quack loudly for several minutes. When we heard the quacking in the office, we knew we were closer to solving a case.

I called Chitty and gave her what I had. A few minutes later she called me back. I could hear the duck quacking in the background as she said, "Woo-hoo! I found him, Sarge!"

I passed this information to my team and then sat down with the sergeant and two detectives from the General Detectives Unit. One of the detectives asked, "How did you get this?"

I replied, "I made a call." I'd always wanted to say something like that.

As we started to discuss a plan, one of the detectives pulled out his cell phone and made his own call. "Hello. Yes, did you email some threats to the governor's office?"

What the fuck was this guy doing?

"Mm-hmm, well, did you think that was a good idea?"

The detective stopped talking. "He hung up on me."

I asked in disbelief, "Did you just call the suspect?"

"Well, yeah."

I spoke slowly. "Do you know where he is?"

He said, "No."

I thought, *No shit, man.*

I asked him, "Do you know if he has access to weapons?"

"No."

"Do you know if he is on his way here or if he is already here?"

"No."

I already knew the answers to all these questions but was trying to make a point. I was pissed, but I didn't have time to be upset, so I let it go. I suggested it would be best to head to the suspect's last known address and attempt to contact him there. Their sergeant agreed. Two detectives left to locate the suspect, and the sergeant told me he would update me once they contacted the suspect.

If they made an arrest, I needed to know immediately. An arrest meant the threat was real and I needed to put some other things into motion. It also meant the possibility of a news story.

7

A short time later, the sergeant called me and let me know they had located and arrested the suspect. He also told me he was preparing a press release.

The last thing I wanted was a press release. I told him I didn't think we needed a press release. Oh man, we went back and forth for about fifteen minutes. We were getting nowhere, so we finally agreed to disagree.

I understood that the sergeant wanted his detectives to get some credit for what they had done. I could respect that. Yes, a press release would show his unit was doing good work, but did it help me or make my team's job any easier? No. I didn't want this in the news for some other person to see and think, *Hey, there are others out there like me. I'm smarter, though. I will succeed.*

I know most people that want to carry out threats do not advertise it in a way that would prevent them from carrying out the threat.

Let's talk assassinations for a quick minute. We know assassins:

- Succeed or fail

- Die or survive

- Are captured or never get caught

- Take credit for what they did or never say a word

It's all over the board for assassins. But for the most part, they do not usually advertise their actions ahead of time. "Assassination of so-and-so coming soon! Like, follow, share, and subscribe for more details."

When an assassin is caught, it can be because:

- They botched the attempt,

- They left clues leading to their capture, or

- They made an error in judgment: They confided in someone they trusted, believing that person was like-minded, but the person wasn't and proceeded to turn them in.

The most dangerous threats are from those that have the capacity to complete their task.

8

It was dark now. I sat in my car thinking about how this press release was not a good idea. I had hit a dead end with the sergeant, so I called the chief. He answered my call saying, "We got him. Great job on working with the general detectives on this one."

"Yes, sir, we did. Chief, I want to talk to you about the press release. I don't like it."

"You don't?"

I went on to explain I felt that a press release would encourage others to threaten the gov. My job was to minimize this type of attention for my principal. The gov had enough to deal with, and this was not something we needed to subject her or her family to. As we continued to talk, I began to realize the chief wanted the press release.

He said, "Don't you think it is good to send the message that if you make threats like this you will be held accountable?"

"Well, sir, he has been arrested. Message sent. I don't think we need to advertise it." I suggested that we have something ready and if the news ran with it, we had a response.

I did not win. The release would be released to the media the next morning after the gov's staff reviewed it. I got it. The chief wanted to show he was protecting his boss, just like the general detective sergeant wanted to show that his detectives were doing a good job. Although I could appreciate the chief's position, I did not feel it was the correct choice.

After the call, I sat in the darkness as I went over a mental checklist of what I had done and what I would need to do the following day. The gov and my team had already been notified of the suspect's arrest. I had already talked with the gov's family, advising them of the nature of the threats and that they were "ugly." The family told me they were used to it. Even so, I knew this would still be difficult to hear.

The following morning, I met with the gov, and we discussed the release. She asked me what I thought. I did not share that I disagreed with my chief. Instead, I told her the upside was we would be ahead of the media and could better manage the information. I told her I had already talked to her family. She thanked me.

The release hit. The news got ahold of the probable cause statement, which included the threats. As expected, the threats were unsettling to hear, especially for the gov's family.

9

The day after the press release, Mary called me in to meet with the gov. The sound in her voice told me this was not going to be a good meeting for me.

Frank was in the gov's office also, standing where I had been during our last meeting with the gov. They stopped talking and both looked up at me as I walked in. Frank and I sat down. The gov was visibly upset.

I have had to testify many times in court, and this reminded me of being cross-examined by defense. The gov was upset with me. She asked about the content of the threats. I could see how they had affected her. I thought, *I messed up, I should have read her the fucking threats.*

I knew she hadn't wanted to hear them, but I knew at that moment me reading them to her would have cushioned the blow. She turned to Frank and asked him if he was aware of the threats that were directed at her family.

"No, Gov. I wasn't."

This was bad.

I was confused. This didn't make sense. Days earlier, Frank had handed me the emails and was briefing the gov's staff. He had been scolded for not notifying me first.

I continued to answer the gov's questions. I remember feeling that if I said anything to the contrary, she might feel I wasn't respecting how she felt. Yes, she was the gov, but she was a mother first. She detailed how I should advise Frank of all matters from this point forward. Yup, this was bad. She had just created a layer between her and me.

When Chief of Staff Frank and I walked out of the office, I stopped him and asked, "Frank, you didn't know about the threats? You handed them to me. You briefed me and your staff."

He said, "No. I didn't know about all of them."

I drove over to the GA building, where I had worked as the mail boy. I met with the chief and advised him on what had happened. In the coming days I felt the gov needed time to cool off. The chief thought differently. He checked in with me and asked if I had resolved things with the gov. He told me to go talk to her and get it settled.

I scheduled some time with the gov the following day.

10

When I arrived at the gov's office, I had to wait about five minutes before she was ready for me. As I waited outside her office, I could see she was reading at her desk. She finally called Mary and told her she was ready to see me. As I approached, she continued to read. I chose to stand this time for what seemed like an eternity but was probably more like a minute or two before Gov put down what she was reading and looked at me.

I asked her, "Gov, are we okay?"

She answered, "I don't know. I need more time to think about that."

I told her, "I know my job is to protect you and your family from harm. That includes all types of harm. I feel I failed here because we are talking about this instead of you focusing on more important things than me." She sat quietly and listened.

"Something I have learned so far in life is everyone has an agenda. My time here with you has been no different. People have their own agendas. They aren't all bad, but most are self-serving.

"I only have one agenda, and that is to keep you and your family safe. When I chose to take this job, I made the decision to protect you as if you were my own family. I am sorry that I failed at that.

"If me being here is affecting you in a way that keeps you from focusing on what you need to do, I should leave." She said nothing. I continued, "I'm not saying I want to leave. I don't. There is no one better suited for this job than me. I am saying if I am a distraction, then I should not be here."

Her shoulders dropped, she removed her glasses, and said, "Carlos, I know your heart." She then turned back to what she had been reading and said, "I just need more time."

"Okay. Thank you for your time, Gov."

As I walked out of her office, I wondered if the gov was glad we had had the talk. I didn't think so. I feared I'd helped make her decision to get rid of me easier.

I updated the chief, who said, "Good. I have time with the gov later this afternoon."

11

Later that afternoon I received a call from one of my detail members. He said, "Big man is here." That meant the chief was there.

I said, "Let me know when he leaves."

"Yup."

The way I saw it was if the chief called me that night, it meant things had been resolved and I would stay on the team. If I didn't get a call, I was out.

About thirty minutes later my phone buzzed. "Big man just left."

I did not get a call from the chief.

12

The next morning, I woke up a few hours earlier than usual. I put on my only black suit, a white shirt, a black tie, and black shoes. I was not going to a gala.

I drove to WSP headquarters, parked, and waited in my car for the call. When my phone rang, it was Annie, the chief's admin assistant. "Hi, Annie! I'll be right there."

A few minutes later I walked into Annie's office. I had visions of the day I had delivered the letter I'd written about my brother-in-law David to Chief Bruett, the one where I first said I wanted to be a trooper. Same room, different pictures.

"Chief is waiting for you. Go on in."

I told myself, *Breathe*, and walked into his office.

The chief was standing in front of his desk talking to one of his assistant chiefs (ACs). His eyes were sad. "Thanks for coming in, Carlos," he said, reaching out his hand to shake mine. Before he released my hand, he said, "It's not going to work." He seemed disappointed—not in me, but in the situation. He motioned for me to sit at the table with the AC.

I felt sick. Why did I feel sick? I had known this was coming.

I said, "Sorry you had to make this decision, Chief. What's next?"

The chief looked surprised. "I didn't think you would respond like this." He went on to explain that he'd once had to remove a trooper from the detail a while back, and that guy had been angry. To me, that meant the trooper didn't know what his role was.

13

The protection detail is about the mission, not the person carrying out the mission. Simple concept. If you can't take the ego out of it, then this isn't the job for you. Now don't get me wrong. I cared about my team, but part of my job was also helping them understand that this job was not about them.

The job was and still is thankless. Nobody knows what you do behind the scenes when you are on the detail, and they shouldn't, not really. Our job was to make everything seem easy and to navigate all the problems without anybody knowing there were problems. This applied to me as well. As much as I was hurt that I was out, I knew this job wasn't about me.

"Well, Chief, it isn't my choice. Whoever is in the red brick house [our nickname for the governor's mansion] should have who they feel comfortable with. I'm just sorry it didn't work out."

The chief thanked me. He and the AC began to explain that my first option was to go back to IAD, since that was where I'd come from. WestNET was in IAD, but since that position was now filled, they offered me a position dealing with asset seizure.

I thought, *Fuck that.* The asset seizure position was being eliminated in about six months anyway. I told them if I had my choice, I would like to go back to a narcotics task force or go back to the road working in King County.

The AC clarified, "You want to go back and supervise troopers rather than go to a position where you don't have to supervise anybody?"

I remember being a little bit offended by his question because I preferred to work rather than drive a desk in a position that was being eliminated.

"Yes, sir. I'm still a trooper. I knew when I took this position I could be back in a white car. My uniform still fits."

I regretted saying that instantly. These guys were living large. No way they could fit in the same uniform that they'd graduated in. I quickly continued so they didn't have time to be offended, "If you need me back in IAD, I will do it. I just would rather go somewhere I could be of better service. I have been fortunate enough to do a lot of things in my career. I want to share that knowledge with others. I think I could pass that on to troopers just like others have done for me. I know my abilities, and I am confident that when another narcotics position opens, I will get it. If you need me somewhere else, though, I will do it."

That was it. The deed was done.

The chief asked me who I thought would be a good fit to replace me. I told him it didn't matter what we thought, it was up to the gov. I thought the gov would want one of my team members for the job. We discussed the pros and cons and then I left. As I walked out, I called my former detail. I told them I was out, but everything would be fine.

Next I called Patrick. I wanted him to hear it from me. I was nervous because this was embarrassing. Patrick had trusted me to do something, and I had failed. He told me he was sorry. I could hear the guilt in his voice. He felt responsible.

He said, "I'm sorry I asked you to do this. You had a good spot where you were."

I said, "It was my choice, not yours. I said yes."

When people asked me why I left, I told them, "It wasn't for me," which was true. I left out the part that I hadn't left on my own terms. This was the first time someone didn't want me for something, and that hurt.

14

About a week later, the president and vice president of the WSP Trooper's Association visited me at my new assignment. I was in Bremerton, Washington, not King County. They looked like two car salesmen stuffed in tight suit pants and oversized jackets. Two more examples of not being able to fit into their original uniforms.

We sat in my new office. I said, "What's this about?"

The president said, "We heard what happened. We want to know if there is anything we can do to help. Can you tell us more about what happened?"

I wasn't going to tell these guys shit. Plus, this wasn't a big deal. "It wasn't for me; the position didn't work out. Thank you for making the trip to see me."

"Are you sure?"

"If you are looking for a disgruntled employee, that isn't me. I'm not sure what you heard or why you are here, but I am fine."

We said our goodbyes and they left.

15

About nine years later I was asked to go back to the gov detail. It was a different team and a different administration. I didn't want to do it, but sometimes you get a tap on the shoulder, and you just do it. This was one of those times.

The chief was glad I was going back to the detail. He told me he had hated what had happened the first time.

I said, "Chief, that's rearview now. Besides, everything worked out for the best." I thought about my black suit and said, "Chief, I don't know if you noticed, but the day you told me it wasn't going to work, I was dressed in all black."

"I did not. Why is that?"

I said, "You know, for my funeral."

He sat in silence and looked like he didn't know what to say. I don't think he thought it was as funny as I did. Then he said, "I'm glad you are back. You get to close this chapter in your career."

He was right. Although I felt defeated from my first experience on the detail, it helped prepare me for what would be the most difficult, yet rewarding, assignment of my career.

"THINGS ARE DIFFERENT NOW."

1

On August 21, 2012—three months after I started at MECTF—I was eating a Cadbury Fruit & Nut bar in my kitchen. Halfway through the chocolate bar, I felt the familiar vibration of my phone. I wiped the chocolate off my fingers and saw it was a text from Bill, who worked on the MECTF.

We worked 4/10s—that's four ten-hour shifts a week. I was scheduled to work Tuesday through Friday, but this was a Monday. Even though I was on a day off, I was never truly off. I went in whenever I was needed. My new lieutenant, Ron Mead, knew this. He also knew I used to keep a cot in my office when I worked at WestNET. He used to tell me, "This isn't WestNET, and don't let me catch you sleeping on a cot in your office."

Ron never found me sleeping on a cot in my office, but it doesn't mean I never slept in that office.

Bill's text said, *Call me.*

I called Bill. "Hey, it's Los. What's up?"

"We got a bad one today. It's a cybertip. Los, it's bad."

"Okay. I can be in the office in about an hour."

"No, we can talk about it tomorrow."

"Bill, I can come in if it's that bad."

I mean, shit. I knew it had to be truly awful since all our cases were bad. Bill told me to enjoy my day and that he would update me the next day, so I didn't go in.

2

The cybertip had originated from NCMEC. They maintain a reporting system called the CyberTipline. It is the nation's centralized reporting system for the online exploitation of children. The public and electronic service providers can make reports of suspected online enticement of children for sexual acts, child sexual molestation, CSAM, child sex tourism, child sex trafficking, unsolicited obscene materials sent to a child, misleading domain names, and misleading words or digital images on the internet.

NCMEC sends these cybertips to the Internet Crimes Against Children (ICAC) Task Force Program. The ICAC is a national network of sixty-one coordinated task forces representing more than 5,400 federal, state, and local law enforcement and prosecutorial agencies. The ICAC program was developed in response to the increasing number of children and teenagers using the internet and other technology, the proliferation of child sexual abuse images available electronically, and the heightened online activity by predators seeking unsupervised contact with potential underage victims. The ICAC Task Force agencies are engaged in both proactive and reactive investigations, forensic examinations, and criminal prosecutions.

ICAC Task Force agencies investigate these cybertips themselves or they distribute them to ICAC affiliates. The affiliates are agencies that have signed a memorandum of understanding (MOU) with the ICAC program. MECTF is an ICAC affiliate.

The next morning, I was the first one into work. I went to my office and closed the door.

My office was bleak, to say the least. On one wall near my desk was a small whiteboard, and on another were two framed collages of my family—one of my kids and me, and the other with photos of me with Julie. The rest of the walls were empty. I had written the word "FOUNDATION" on the whiteboard. Below it I wrote a list of things I felt we needed to become an actual task force:

- Dedicated funding

- Admin support

- Training

- Donations via website

- More detectives

- Task Force Officer (TFO) status

- An MECTF in every district

On my desk was a manila envelope with the words "Sgt. Rodriguez" written on it. Inside was the cybertip, about twenty pages thick. I began to read. This was bad, really bad.

Words turned to visions. Visions to disgust. Disgust brought along his friend sadness. Sadness left and was replaced by anger.

3

The cybertip was from a social media company that owned a social application that provided a way for its users to connect with people who have similar interests. Users could upload photos, create profiles, and communicate through live video streams. The company had reviewed a troubling chat conversation between two of its users and reported it to NCMEC.

"Morgan," was a twenty-year-old single mother of a six-month-old baby boy. She connected with "MikeD," who was also twenty and single. MikeD didn't have his own children, but he was interested in children. They began to chat and quickly learned they had a lot in common, including some taboo desires and experiences.

Taboo desires are ones that are not necessarily accepted by society, but that doesn't mean they are illegal. This was not the case for Morgan and MikeD. Their conversations were about incest, bestiality, and sex with children, which are definitely illegal. MikeD detailed how he had molested and raped both of his younger siblings. His brother was seventeen years old, and his sister was eleven. He also detailed how he'd had sex with animals on his parents' property.

Morgan told MikeD she had experience with incest as well. She sent MikeD a sexually explicit image of her and her infant son that she had taken herself.

Although they lived nearly two hours from each other, they arranged to meet in person. According to their chats, MikeD met with Morgan and her son at the end of July 2012.

I thought, *Oh God, it's August.*

Bill was right. This was a bad one.

I'm glad I was alone when I read the cybertip. I wasn't ready for it. Questions raced through my mind. *What happened to the baby when they met? How many times did they meet? How many other people has she done this with? Where are his sister, his brother, the little baby boy? Are they okay?*

Were they okay?

This question still haunts me. Were they okay? Are they okay? The answer is, I don't know. I worked these cases and, once my part was done, there were so many that we had to move on to the next case.

I wondered what made these two people want to commit such crimes. What had happened to them? They were so young.

Remember, at this point in my career I was still new to investigating crimes against children and had only helped with a few cases. This was my first real introduction into working child exploitation cases.

I stopped reading the tip and placed my hands on my desk, palms down. I slid my palms forward, and the coldness of the desk felt good as it spread to my forearms. I put the cybertip back into the manila envelope. My throat was locked. I tried to speak, but my voice didn't want to come out of my mouth. I swallowed a few times and then practiced saying a few words out loud so I could call Bill.

He answered, "Carlito."

I used to hate when people called me that name. It's not my name, after all. Now I don't care. I don't sweat the small shit anymore.

"You clear for traffic?"

He said, "Yes."

"This is bad, man. I don't know how things were run around here before, but we needed to move on this yesterday. We need to find this kid."

4

I'm sure my predecessors worked hard, but not at the pace I was used to. They hadn't carried a caseload; I did. Also, this wasn't our only case. Bill was working another high-profile case, so I worked this case with my other detective. We will call him Jeff. He was from a city agency and not as intense or as active as Bill.

Working these types of cases affects people differently. Some may be on the task force for too long, and others are not as motivated as Bill or me. To this day I don't know how it affected Jeff, but I do know he didn't care for my supervisory style or my questions. And my questions were basic ones such as, "What are you doing?" and "Where are you?"

Right now, that didn't matter. Jeff was still a good person and cared about kids, and his strongest skill was his interviewing.

Jeff and I came up with a plan. We wanted to find the mother and the baby first, then MikeD. We had two addresses in two different cities for Morgan. The farther city was Aberdeen, which was nearly two hours away from us. The second was Montesano, which was closer but still about an hour away. Aberdeen is a logging town, and Montesano is much smaller. If you blink you will miss the exit. We decided to go to Aberdeen first and then hit Montesano on the way back. The address in Aberdeen was a dead end, so we drove to Montesano.

Once there, we started to surveil a house that sat on a slight slope above the main road. We parked across the street and watched for Morgan.

While we were watching the house, Jeff called a police officer he knew from the area. It turned out the police officer knew the landlord of the house. Jeff called the landlord, but there was no answer. He left her a message. We saw no movement at the house, so we decided to call it a day and start again early the next morning.

5

I was on edge when I got home, and Julie could tell. We were lying in bed next to each other, her watching *Friends* reruns while I tried to fall asleep.

"Is something wrong?" she asked. "You are acting weird."

I didn't tell her about the case. I just said, "Yeah, we have a tough case and I'm just thinking about it is all. I may be home late tomorrow."

She gave a quick smile and said, "Okay. I love you."

"I love you too, honey."

We kissed each other and then I turned away from her. She went back to watching Ross and Rachel, and I eventually fell asleep. If I could go back, I would tell the younger me, "Hug her. You need to hug her more."

Back then I didn't realize how hard it must have been to be married to me. I was a lot to deal with. I mean, imagine your loved one not always being there when you need them but always being available for others. It takes a special person to deal with that. Julie was my special person. She was there for me whenever I needed her, and I chose a profession that took me away from her. There were a lot of times when I was home, but I didn't share how I was feeling in an attempt to keep her separated from that world. I didn't take the time to think about how she may have processed that. I know I thanked her, but I didn't thank her enough.

When I came home, I did what I needed to decompress, but I didn't always think of what she needed, which wasn't much at all. Even though I was physically home with my family, I wasn't truly there. In my head I was working a case. I share this because if you are married and doing this work, please take the time to be present with your partner—fully present. They sacrifice a lot for you.

If your partner does this work, I want to tell you it isn't something you did or didn't do when they don't seem like they are fully present. They most likely are processing some difficult things. For me, I kept my emotions boxed up and didn't tell my family how this work made me feel. I had a hard time with that.

I felt I was protecting them, but in reality, I was distancing myself from those that loved me the most. Speaking with them about it now, I realize that at times they felt it was something they had done, or they perceived that I didn't want to spend time with them. I regret that.

6

The next morning, we learned Morgan lived at the house in Montesano. I remember being anxious as we drove back down, hoping to find Morgan and the baby boy.

Jeff and I decided to make contact at the house. A teenage boy answered the door. He examined the badges hanging around our necks through his thick black-framed glasses. It wasn't cold out, but the boy was wearing a dark unzipped puffy jacket over a white T-shirt, gym shorts, and white crew socks. No shoes. His jacket stopped halfway down his gym shorts.

"Can I help you?" His voice sounded like it lived in his nose.

Jeff said, "I hope so. We are looking for Morgan. Is she home?"

The boy said, "She is not. What do you want with my sister?"

The boy continued with his questions before Jeff could answer.

"May I ask what this is about? I also know from shows such as *CSI* and *Law and Order* that you need a search warrant to enter my residence, or any residence for that matter. Do either of you have a search warrant?"

Jeff said, "No, we do not. Is your mom or dad home?"

He said, "Well then, you cannot enter my residence. We can continue to talk with each other right here if you would like, and no, my mom is not home."

Jeff said, "Do you like *CSI*?"

"Yes, I do. I also know most of the time when police officers contact a residence and ask for someone, they don't always tell the truth about why they want to speak with that person."

Jeff said, "You know *CSI* is a TV show?"

"Yes, I do know that it is a television show. It is quite accurate from what I have read."

Jeff said, "Yeah, and we solve all of our crimes in an hour, just like on *CSI*."

The boy looked at Jeff and then at me. He squinted his eyes a bit and his mouth bent slightly into a smile. He said, "I see what you did there. Actually, once you subtract the number of commercials it is closer to thirty minutes."

The boy had jokes.

As Jeff talked to the boy, I wondered how the kid could stand being in his jacket in August. He eventually told us Morgan had gone to the store with her baby.

We relayed this information to the Montesano PD. Within

minutes they located Morgan on a city bus with her son. Morgan and her baby were transported to the PD.

We said our goodbyes to the boy and headed to the PD. They let us use a small office to interview Morgan. The three of us sat together at a small table. Her son sat in a car seat that she placed on the floor next to her.

Jeff said hello to Morgan and asked her if we could speak with her. She agreed. Jeff advised Morgan of her rights and a waiver of rights. She sat motionless in her chair and listened to Jeff. When he finished, she told him she understood her rights, and she again agreed to speak with us.

7

Jeff was what we called the "one," and I was the "two" for this interview. That meant Jeff would ask most of the questions and I would take notes. The notes were mostly a list of questions that I wanted to ask. If Jeff asked the question or Morgan answered it, then I would cross it off my list.

When Jeff was done asking questions, he would ask me if I had anything for Morgan. This method worked well for us, especially since we had not interviewed with each other yet. Even if we had, I liked this method because no matter how well you think you know your partner, you don't always know where their line of questioning is going. If your partner interrupts, it can swing the interview in a totally different direction.

Morgan told us she'd grown up in a household where familial sex was "normal." She didn't learn her family life was different until one day while she was at school. She was at recess and started to tell some of her classmates how her stepdad "tucked her in" each night.

One of her classmates pulled her away from the group, saying, "Don't talk about that here. Not everyone here is like us. Your dad will get in trouble."

Until that moment, Morgan thought what her stepdad did was what all kids experienced at home. It was her normal.

Morgan spoke with Jeff as if he was her only friend. She was enjoying herself. She answered all of Jeff's questions without hesitating. If she didn't understand a question, she would ask for clarification and then continue talking with him.

As the conversation continued, Jeff asked Morgan about a photo she had taken with her son. It was the photo from the cybertip. Doing this work there are some images that are seared into my brain. No matter how much I want them gone, they don't go away. This is one of those images.

In the photo Morgan was placing her son's foot into her vagina.

Jeff asked, "How did that happen?"

"I don't know. It just fell in," she said, laughing the kind of laugh someone does when they are nervous but don't want you to know it.

Jeff said, "Okay. Fell in?"

"Yes."

"Why did you take a picture of it?"

"I thought it was kind of funny. So I took a picture." Again, she laughed.

Jeff asked about her experiences with bestiality. Morgan looked down at the table and then back up at Jeff. "Sometimes my dog licks me."

"Licks you?"

"Yes. When I use the bathroom, sometimes he cleans me." My face strained to conceal my discomfort. She smiled. "Not all the time. It just happens sometimes. I bend over and he just does it."

"Okay. How often would you say that happens?"

"Whenever I run out of toilet paper."

8

The focus of the conversation shifted to MikeD. Morgan told us she'd met him in Spanaway, an area just south of Tacoma, and assured us that MikeD hadn't done anything with her son.

I thought, *Sure, just like your son's foot "fell" into your vagina.*

She told us she thought MikeD lived close to where they met in Spanaway.

I told myself, *We have to find this guy.*

Morgan was booked into the Grays Harbor County Jail. Her son was taken into protective custody and later released to a family member from Oregon. Morgan's brother continued to live with their mother. There was no evidence that Morgan had offended on him.

Once Morgan left the room, Jeff's shoulders dropped. We both raised our eyebrows while pressing our lips together. Jeff and I had our differences, but I was proud of him. Interviewing people about this shit takes a lot out of you. When you finish, it's like taking off a fifty-pound rucksack after a ten-mile hike.

I asked him, "You good?"

Jeff said, "Yeah, I'm good."

We began our one-hour drive back to our office. We didn't talk much about the interview. I think we had heard enough. Once we made it to the office, we said our goodbyes for the night and planned on meeting early the next day to find MikeD.

9

"I'm good." I heard and said that more times than I can remember. "I'm good." That's what we told each other. Sometimes I said it because I didn't want to talk about whatever I was being asked about. Other times I was "good" so I could focus on what was next. I can hear my mom's voice telling me, "Mijo, you control your emotions. Your emotions don't control you." *Okay, Mom, I'll pack them away.*

I became an expert at packing boxes and a master of disassociation. It was mandatory for me to think, to function.

Police officers are trained to assess threats, implement solutions, and sometimes go toward the danger. We are expected to choose the safety of others over our own. When I'm in danger, time slows down like a movie; at least that's how it feels. My first fight as a trooper with a DUI at a Seattle PD precinct—slow motion. Rolling up on my first fatal scene with bodies lying in multiple lanes of the freeway—slow motion. The first time on a traffic stop realizing, *Fuck, I might have to shoot this guy*—so slow. It was my body's way of recalling what I had learned and then applying it. Did time actually slow down? Of course not. All these scenarios were fast-paced and lasted only a few minutes. Sometimes only a few seconds.

"I'm good" translated into no longer having the capacity to feel sad. I didn't even cry when my dog Diego died. I forgot what it was like. I asked myself, *Who does that?* I thought there was something wrong with me.

When I retired, my need to compartmentalize things wasn't as frequent, but the most random things triggered me. Seeing a discarded cup of noodles in a yard. A statue in a restaurant. The smell of maple syrup. The phrase "It is what it is." Simple things.

I had difficulty maintaining my composure at times. I made up excuses to be alone in order to cope. It was my way of keeping others from detecting that I was damaged.

"I need to take this call."

"Hey, I'll catch up, I forgot something in my car."

"Excuse me, I need to go to the restroom."

There was no call, I hadn't forgotten anything, and I didn't need to use the restroom. I had to escape. I needed a break to figure it out, to breathe, to hide the tremble in my left hand. I excused myself because I was embarrassed, ashamed.

Today, I know it is okay to feel these things and I am better for it. Yes, it has taken me some time to heal and manage my emotions, but I know if something breaks me, I will heal. I will ultimately be more resilient. I am in a good place now, and these experiences have allowed me to help others in different ways.

I believe when you experience traumatic circumstances, you bring the trauma with you. It redefines who you are. Although it's easy to lose oneself in the process, it doesn't mean you have to. I am who I am because of everything I have experienced. Even the shit I want to forget.

I didn't take the steps to process how this affected me back then. I ignored it. I didn't respect the gravity of it all. I made the choice to manage my pain on my own, which was a mistake—a mistake you can avoid.

10

All we had to go on was the name MikeD, a selfie he had shared with Morgan, and that he might live in or near Spanaway. We contacted the Department of Licensing (DOL) and requested all photos for persons named Mike with the last name starting with a D who was in his early twenties and within a five-mile radius of Spanaway. If we didn't locate him, we would expand the radius.

The plan was to compare MikeD's selfie against the DOL photos. At that time we did not have access to any type of facial recognition software. This meant we had to compare the photos one by one until we found him.

We asked Ruby from our Missing and Unidentified Persons Unit to assist us. Ruby was a quiet woman and didn't say much. She loved helping us, though. A few hours later Ruby knocked on my open office door. "Sergeant Rodriguez?" Ruby handed me a DOL return and said, "I found him."

I looked at the photo and it stared back with dead eyes. It was him. I thought, *We got you, fucker.*

MikeD was associated with two residences. One was a large property with a house and several outbuildings in Tacoma near the WSP district office. The other house was about five miles to the north in an area of Tacoma called Parkland.

Like I explained before, we didn't have many resources, so I asked for help. HTCU gave me some detectives, but it would take a while to get everyone together. One HTCU detective and I were first to the area.

I had the HTCU detective set up at the house near our district office. This location was difficult to surveil due to large pine trees and overgrown brush. The detective was limited to the monitoring of who came and went from the residence.

I set up on the Parkland house, a basic split-entry home. I parked across the street with several cars for cover. There were no cars in the driveway, but that didn't mean the house was empty. We kept an eye out for MikeD while we waited for Bill and the other detectives.

Jeff was posted at a nearby PD and was working on the affidavit for a search warrant. When I worked at WestNET, we would just get the warrant over the phone. Thing is, Jeff had never done a telephonic search warrant and seemed stressed about doing it for the first time on this case.

I thought, *The best way to learn is to do it*, but I didn't press the matter. I wanted him to stay focused on the case and not be stressed about doing something new.

A few minutes after I set up on the Parkland house, a car pulled into the driveway. It was MikeD. The hair on my arms stood at attention. Excitement and nervousness filled me all at once.

MikeD exited his car and walked to the front door of the house. His shoulder pressed a phone to his ear as he searched for his keys. I hoped it was an iPhone. We knew MikeD used an iPhone to communicate with Morgan.

I need that phone. I called the detective at the other house. "I have eyes on him. What's the ETA for the others to get to you?"

"They're almost here, Los."

"I'll call Jeff then check back with you. If they get there before I call back, leave one there to keep eyes on. Bring at least one with you."

I called Jeff and advised him we were going to contact the residence and see if we could get MikeD to come out of the home.

11

When I was on my way to set up surveillance on MikeD's house, I had noticed a collision at a nearby intersection. MikeD had come from the same area as the collision. I decided to use a ruse by telling MikeD someone had given us his license plate, saying he had witnessed the collision. My hope was MikeD would exit the residence with his iPhone. A ruse is a tactic used by law enforcement. Under existing laws, officers are permitted to use a ruse—a statement an officer knows is not true—in limited circumstances.

About twenty minutes later, two detectives met up with me. We had a uniformed trooper with a fully marked patrol car with us as well. After a quick briefing we headed to the house.

One detective rode with me, followed by the other detective, who was followed by the marked unit. I pulled into the driveway and parked behind MikeD's car.

Two of us approached the front door. We were wearing black jackets, polo shirts, and jeans. The jackets had hidden pockets that concealed panels with a cloth badge on the front of the jacket and the word *Detective* on the back. We removed the panels from their pockets so the badges and words were visible. We wore ballistic vests underneath the jackets. We also hung our metal badges around our necks. There was no mistaking that we were law enforcement officers. The marked unit parked on the street in front of the house where he was visible from the front door.

There were several steps leading up to the front porch. To the left of the front door was a window that was at knee level when standing on the porch. It was frosted so most likely belonged to a bathroom.

The approach to a house was the most nerve-racking part of contacting a residence for me. I often wondered, *Is someone going to shoot me from a window or at the front door? How many people are really in there?*

I stood at the door and the other detective stood to the left of the window that was at our knees. I knocked three times. No answer. I knocked a little bit harder—harder than a knock, but not quite a pound.

The detective pointed at the frosted window to the left of the door. "Sarge, I think someone is in there."

I moved over, as I didn't want to be caught standing in front of the doorway while looking at the window. Doorways, stairwells, hallways, and entryways are known as fatal funnels—choke points or areas that can lead to being injured or killed. You may be able to see what's coming for you but unable to get out of harm's way.

I tapped on the window, and it opened immediately. Steam rolled out, revealing MikeD wearing nothing but a bath towel. I could hear the shower running behind him. I don't know how he didn't hear me knocking on the door. Most likely he did hear me.

As I grabbed the badge around my neck and showed it to him, I quickly scanned the room. The mirror was covered with condensation from the shower. His right hand was empty. I couldn't see his left hand.

"Hi. Can I see your hands, please?" He complied. His hands were empty.

He appeared older than twenty. By the looks of him he didn't spend much time in the sun. His hair was shorter than in his photos but still had some curl to it. He wasn't wet, so I knew he hadn't made it into the shower yet. His eyes looked dead, just like in his DOL photo. He said nothing.

"Thanks for that. I get nervous when I can't see someone's hands. Can you please keep them here on the windowsill?"

MikeD placed both of his hands on the windowsill and left them there.

"I'm Sergeant Rodriguez with the Washington State Patrol. We are investigating a collision, and one of the witnesses gave us your license plate. They said you witnessed the accident. I want to talk to you and ask a few questions if that's okay."

He looked right through me.

I have contacted hundreds of people as a police officer and even more throughout my life. When I meet someone, they show me some sort of emotion or reaction, especially when they are meeting with the police. Most people display some discomfort or fear, unless they want the police to do something for them. If they want something, then it's usually a sense of urgency, joy, or relief. I was expecting discomfort, fear, or even confusion from MikeD.

He gave me nothing. This time I was the one confused. I was the uncomfortable one.

MikeD said plainly, "Yes. I saw the accident."

"Great! It would help us a lot. Is there anyone else inside there with you?"

"No. I am alone."

"Okay, we will wait here for you."

As I spoke with him, I continued to look past him, searching for anything that could hurt us. I didn't see any weapons or objects he might decide to use as a weapon, but I couldn't see past the room he was standing in. A few minutes later a fully dressed MikeD met us at the front door. His hands were still empty. He was thin and about three inches taller than me.

MikeD stepped outside and closed the door behind him. I couldn't see anything inside of the house.

I asked him again, "You are alone, right? Nobody else in there?"

He said, "I am alone." I hoped that was the truth.

I smiled and asked, "Do you have your phone with you?" Usually when I smile at someone, they give me a smile, even if it's forced. No smile. Same eyes.

"I don't have a phone."

"You don't have a phone?"

"No."

"Don't you have an iPhone?"

MikeD rubbed the pad of his thumb in circles against the pad of his index finger. "I used to. I lost it."

"That's weird. I was out here when you parked your car, I was right over there. You looked like you were on the phone. An iPhone."

He started to rub all his fingers with his thumb like he was feeling a piece of fabric. He said nothing.

"Do you want to go and get it?"

"I don't want to talk anymore. I think I need an attorney."

I knew as soon as the words left my mouth: I had pushed too hard. *Fuck.*

I took my matte black Peerless handcuffs out of my back pocket. They were not my standard issue cuffs but were from my time at WestNET. They were black so if my cuffs were left at the jail, I could tell which cuffs were mine. I had etched a small X into them for added insurance.

The cuffs clicked as I secured MikeD's hands behind his back. I placed him in the back of the marked patrol car. Before I shut the door, I leaned closer to him and said, "I met your friend Morgan. I have your chats. We know everything."

12

Did we know everything? Absolutely not. Did it feel good saying we knew everything? Fuck yes, it did.

This was not ideal. A suspect talking is always better than silence. In this line of work, conversations are where it's at. Even if it isn't the truth. I can work with lies and denials. When a suspect doesn't say anything, it can make things difficult.

In this case, it didn't matter. We had enough to arrest him, and he had lied about his iPhone. That was a win for us.

A judge granted Jeff a search warrant for both locations. We left eyes on the second location while we processed the Parkland home.

Four detectives and I cleared the house. We had a marked unit and a few other officers on perimeter. That means we had cops posted on each side of the residence. The home was a split level, so one of us held the stairs going up to the main level and the other four cleared the bottom level. When they were done, we did the same on the main level. No one else was in the home.

When we searched a residence, we would set up an evidence processing station. I assigned one detective to the station. It wasn't elaborate, usually a small table and materials to package evidence. As detectives searched areas, they brought any evidence they had located to the evidence processing station where it was packaged and recorded. During the search, one of the detectives called me to MikeD's bedroom. "Sarge, look at this. I found it under his bed."

He was holding a small wooden box about the size of a brick of Philadelphia cream cheese, held closed with a small brass-colored latch. Inside was a letter from MikeD's sister along with a pair of her panties. The letter described how she missed him since he had moved out of his parents' house and wished that they could be together.

After that, most of us remained quiet, speaking only when we needed to. We continued to locate and gather evidence, and yes, we located his iPhone and other digital media.

MikeD's siblings lived with his father at the other location. We learned his parents knew he was abusing his sister. They told the little girl, "That is a sin. Ask God for forgiveness." Wonderful parenting skills.

His brother and sister were taken into protective custody, but eventually they went back to their parents. A forensic examination of MikeD's digital devices revealed he had created CSAM of his little sister. This was good for the case, but the reality of it hurt my heart.

13

When I became a state trooper, I started to have dreams. Nightmares really. It usually happened when I was stressed out or something bothered me.

When I was brand-new, my dreams were about someone trying to kill me, which turned into me having to shoot them to stay alive. The dreams varied. Sometimes someone would shoot at me and my gun was too heavy to pull out of my holster. Before the bullet hit me, I would wake up. Other times I could get my gun out, but the trigger wouldn't move when I pulled it. Sometimes I could pull the trigger, but the bullet would either expand in the barrel, never making it out of the gun, or the bullet would simply fall on the ground. You get the picture.

When I started working crimes against children, my dreams became much different. The most frequent dream was of me walking down a road alone. In the dream I am not in my body; it's like I'm watching a movie, and I'm the person on the screen. The road is in a rural area with one lane each way but no lane markers. No shoulders. No cars. No animals. No other people, just me.

My walking would turn into a light jog and then gradually into a sprint. I would watch as my body slowly lifted off the ground. I would begin to float upward into the sky. I was watching myself, but I could feel everything as if it were me, because, well, it was me.

I would be anxious but amused at the same time. I would float up and then back down to the ground again. First ten feet up. Next, it was twenty. I would bound up and down like an astronaut walking on the moon.

Then the dream would change. I would continue to float up but did not come back down. Now I was no longer watching myself but was in my body. As I accelerated up, the earth shrunk below me. I was being pulled upward. My amusement quickly turned to fear.

I would swing at the ground trying to swim back to the earth. The wind was cold through my clothes and on my face. My sight was blurry like when you open your eyes underwater. Higher and higher through the clouds I would go.

Then I would plateau and float in the same spot for a short moment, just enough time to wipe the moisture from my eyes. I could see clearly again and found that I was suspended over patches of farmland sewn together like a quilt. Next, my stomach would drop as I gradually fell back down to the earth. I wasn't in free fall but was accelerating as if something was pushing me. I was terrified and would claw at the sky, but it didn't slow me down. I was screaming, but the screams were silent. I would wake up just before I hit the ground.

I had this dream a lot. It varied slightly each time. Sometimes I floated over empty cities instead of the farmland, but it was pretty much the same thing—me alone with no voice.

The worst dreams are when something happens to one of my kids. I still have these dreams, just not as frequently. In the dream I never witness what happens; it's always afterward. I get home, see a stranger leave my house, and walk inside to find one of my kids in their room sitting on their bed. Sometimes it is my daughter and other times my son—never together in the same dream.

As I enter their room, my child looks up at me but then turns away. I ask them, "Who was that?" but they don't answer me. I then panic on the inside but not on the outside. "What's wrong?" I ask. No response. I know the answer but ask anyway. "Did they hurt you?"

The panic fights to escape, but I keep it inside. It has to stay inside so they don't know I am losing my mind.

This dream is always the same. My daughter or son looks away from me and down, not really focused on anything.

When I call their name, I see they have tears on their face. They get up and come to me with their arms down in front of them, their palms toward me. We hug, and I tell them it's all right and not their fault. Then I wake up.

If someone is in bed with me when I wake up, I ask them to hold me. Then I tell myself it's not real and eventually go back to sleep.

14

This case with Morgan and MikeD left me feeling the same as in those dreams—helpless.

I broke down for the first time working this case. Three months in and I was already breaking. It happened after I finished listening to MikeD's eleven-year-old sister describe what he had done to her. After listening to her interview, I had to get outside.

I could hear my mom saying, "Mijo, walk fast. People will think you have somewhere important to be even if you don't." I walked as quickly as I could, trying not to look panicked. I was just about to step off the sidewalk and into the parking lot when Lieutenant Mead called me wanting an update.

My voice hurt like I had strep throat; it gave out. I cleared my throat. "Hey, L.T., she disclosed." I remember telling him that this was why we did this job. When a child discloses what happened to them, it's a weird feeling. Yes, it is horrible, but let me explain. When a child discloses, it means we have the evidence needed to hold a bad person accountable for a terrible act. It means we can build a case to hopefully keep a bad person from harming a child again. So, in a weird, fucked-up way we were happy when we got a disclosure. But the happiness based on a child sharing how they were tormented faded quickly. It was followed by guilt. Fucked up, right?

My lieutenant had a few more questions. As we talked, I stepped off the yellow-painted curb and then back up onto the curb again. The rhythm of this repeated action soothed me. I cleared the call, took a final step off the curb, and got in my car. I reached for the radio, paused for a few seconds, and then drove in silence to the nearest Starbucks.

"Yes. I would like a trenta black iced tea with three pumps of classic."

After I had my tea, I drove home. I turned onto my street and pulled over before going into my driveway. I sat in my car with my eyes closed for what I think was five minutes. I then drove into my driveway and parked in front of our detached garage.

My son was playing in the backyard and saw me pull up. He ran out to me and opened my car door.

"Dad!" His smile made me smile. It still does, every time.

I didn't say anything. I just looked at him.

He grabbed my arm and pulled me out of my car. He hugged me. I don't remember what he said, but seeing him warmed my insides. He took hold of my hand and led me into the house. I love him so much.

15

Morgan and MikeD were arrested in separate counties. This meant two different prosecutors, two different trials, and the potential for two different outcomes.

Morgan was arrested in Grays Harbor County. The prosecutor there was aggressive and willing to go to trial if Morgan didn't accept her offer. Morgan accepted her offer and pled guilty. She was sentenced to ten years to life in prison. At the time of me writing this book she is still in prison.

The prosecutor in Pierce County was not aggressive at all. A better way to describe her would be spineless, but that's my opinion. She preferred to offer deals over going to trial. She agreed to offer MikeD something called a special sex offender sentencing alternative, SSOSA. This meant MikeD would not go to prison.

I was pissed, but it was out of my hands. My part in this case was done. Once we present our cases to the prosecutor's office, it is up to them to make a charging decision. My job was to make sure we conducted a thorough investigation and that I organized my case file so a prosecutor could easily digest the evidence. The better the case you put together, the better chance you have that your case is charged.

Prior to working crimes against children, I didn't care as much if my cases were charged or not. I knew I had done my part, and I moved on to the next thing. These cases were different. I wanted every one of these cases to be charged. If I needed to do more work to get that done, I did it. Set a hoop on fire, and I will jump through it. Like Westley in *The Princess Bride* says, "As you wish."

Some time passed, but eventually MikeD made a mistake. He violated his SSOSA several years later by possessing large amounts of CSAM. He pled guilty before HTCU finished processing his computer and was sentenced to about seven and a half years in prison.

This was a success in most persons' eyes. We removed several children from harm in a small amount of time with minimal resources. Both offenders were in prison. My command staff thanked me and my team for doing a good job. Great job, right? It was, but it didn't feel like one. Yes, I was proud of how we'd come together, but I was disappointed in how few resources we had.

We made it work, but it was not efficient. It was not good enough. Things needed to change.

16

I have been fortunate to have many different roles in my career. Each assignment had its own obstacles to overcome, and I didn't always know what to do. Shit, I still don't know what to do half of the time. I focused on taking care of those around me and asked for help from those I trusted. Things always seemed to pan out.

This was different, though. Working child exploitation cases is so different. It's hard to explain. If you are working or have worked these cases, you get it. No matter how much training investigators receive, nothing prepares them for what they will see and feel doing this type of work.

The trauma I experienced growing up taught me to separate my emotions. It helped me to focus, making me more efficient at doing this job. Like I said before, I brought my experiences with me, and they redefined how I see the world. My lens is forever changed. It helps me focus, but it did not keep me mentally healthy.

Instead, I put on a face and said what I felt were the right things to say. But what I said was not true. Not really. I coped the only way I knew how: Fill a box. Put it on a shelf. New case? New box.

I lost myself in the process. I kept myself busy and focused on protecting others. I worried about keeping those I worked with safe while neglecting myself in the process.

Those of you that do this work are strong-willed. You have to be. That doesn't mean you are invincible, even though you may feel it's expected of you. You are human. It is okay to talk about how you feel and to figure it out. Protect yourself by taking breaks.

I thought, *I don't have time for breaks. There is too much to do.*

I was so wrong. The breaks allow you to keep doing the great work you are meant to do. It's a reset.

It is okay to pack boxes, but remember, you don't have an endless supply of boxes or shelf space. Unpack a few along the way to make room for the new stuff.

NINE

THE TEACUP

1

When I was a kid, the best part of school was the end. I did not like school. Probably because I didn't have many friends growing up. Part of that was because we moved around, since my dad was in the army. Another reason was because I was smaller than the rest of the kids and an introvert. I remember each time we moved to a new place, all the kids already had friends.

Back then I either kept to myself or played with my sister. You see, we were best friends. We did most things together. The bond that other kids had with their friends, I had with my sister. Now we have our own separate lives and don't talk as much, but we still love each other.

When we played together, it was usually us racing each other in our backyard. The race was from one fence line to the next in a large backyard with thick green grass. We would pick one fence line as the starting line and line up next to each other in our best racing stances. I liked to plant one hand on the ground like the racers on

TV. Carmen preferred to stand with karate chop hands—one hand in front and one behind her.

"Reeeaaady . . . seeet . . . go!"

Although I was small for my age, I was still bigger than my sister. Her little legs couldn't keep up with me. As I pulled away from her, she would let out a fake cry. I would stop and turn around to check on her, knowing she wasn't really crying. Her head would be down and her shoulders slumped. I could hear her giggling. She couldn't help it.

I would play along. "What's wrong? Are you okay?"

As soon as I was next to her, she would take off as fast as she could, which was extremely slow. She ran like her shoelaces were tied together in small, even steps. Whenever Carmen ran, her cheeks glazed over and turned a deep tomato red. She looked so sticky. I let her get halfway through the yard before I ran past her.

As I approached the finish line, I could hear her footsteps slow to a walk.

She would say, "Oh no, no, noooo!"

This was my cue to get a cramp, trip on a "log" or a "rock," or simply fall down.

Carmen would win the race. She always won the race. Her celebration consisted of her jogging around in a circle with her little arms raised over her head. Then we did it again. We would run for hours.

2

On this day I had no time to race my sister. It was report card day, and my grades were bad—three D's bad. My teacher sent me home with a manila envelope tied closed with a little red string wrapped around a brown disk. While seated on the school bus,

I unwrapped the red string from the disk and wrapped it tightly around the tip of my pinky finger. It hurt at first, but the pain faded as quickly as the color from the tip of my finger. Once my finger was numb, I unwrapped the red string and let the blood return to my fingertip. I did this a few more times and then wrapped it back around the brown disk.

Inside the envelope was my report card along with a slip for my parents to sign to prove they had seen my three D's.

The bus reached my stop. I exited and walked slowly toward my house. During the short five-minute walk I decided on a plan. My dad would not be home until around 5 p.m., and my mom was always working late. I had time to fix this.

I unlocked the front door of my house and went to my parents' room on the main floor. Sitting in the corner of their room on a small wooden desk was Mom's maroon IBM Selectric typewriter. I pulled open the center drawer of her desk and found paper clips, mechanical pencils, an eraser, and a small red-and-black cardboard box. I removed the lid of the box and dumped out about a dozen metal balls covered with small letters and numbers.

The IBM Selectric was cutting-edge in 1982. You see, it didn't have individual keys with letters and numbers. All the fonts were on a small metal ball about an inch and a half in diameter. Each metal ball had a different font. In order to change the font, one simply had to swap out one ball for another.

I tested ball after ball until I found a B that looked like the other B's on my report card. I decided on B's to replace the D's because they were similar in shape, and I didn't usually get A's. A's would be suspicious.

I slowly rubbed the eraser against the first D and watched as it disappeared. I then inserted the report card into the typewriter.

Resting my index finger on the typewriter's B key, I closed my eyes, waited for a few seconds, and then quickly pressed the key. It fucking worked! Well, at least for the first two B's. They were spot-on.

It was the third B that screwed me. *Motherfucker.* Now I had to erase the new grade. The typewriter had an erase key, but I quickly learned it did not work. I went weak behind my knees and panic started to set in.

I removed the card, picked up the eraser, and started again. The misaligned B started to fade, but the card was now much thinner where the grade had been. About fifteen minutes later the misaligned B was replaced by a new and much darker B in the correct spot. The report card looked great except the area below the three new grades was a lighter blue than the rest of the card, and of course one B was darker than the rest. No turning back now. I placed the card in the envelope with the little slip. I wound the little red string one last time around the brown disk and waited for one of my parents to get home.

I was looking in the fridge for some food when I heard the garage open. I stood in the kitchen and stared at the door that led to the garage, fixated on the brass doorknob. *Please be Dad, please be Dad, please be Dad.* You see, if it was my dad I had a way better shot at pulling this off. I imagined he would look at the card super quick, sign the slip, and then go watch TV.

I could hear car keys scraping on the other side of the door. The knob started to turn, and the door opened. *Dang.*

My mom walked into the kitchen wearing one of her multicolored blouses. She dressed and styled her hair like an eighties news anchor. I remember her always being in business attire. She was five foot three with a round face—not fat round, but still round. She sold term life insurance for a company called A.L. Williams, and most evenings she was working. When I rode in the car with her, she would listen to self-help and negotiation tapes. Sometimes she listened to a TV pastor named Robert Schuller who had a Crystal Cathedral and wore big, thick glasses.

I handed my mother the manila envelope. She unwrapped the red string and removed the blue card. She held the card up in front of her face while still holding the keys to her red 1980 Honda hatchback in the same hand. I watched as she studied the card. She squinted while turning her head slightly to one side. She locked eyes with mine.

Shit.

She put the card and her keys on the kitchen counter, cleared her throat, and said calmly, "Carlos, go to your room. Do not play with your toys. Sit on your bed and wait for me. I need to put some things away."

This was not new to me. I figured my failed attempt would result in three swats with a wooden paddle. Although I didn't like it, this was easy work.

The paddle was a custom job my mom had made at a woodshop when we lived in Germany. It had a slender handle that widened into the "contact zone." It reminded me of an oar, but with a short handle. My mom took my sister and me to the woodshop when she had it made. We were excited about going to the woodshop, until we learned the paddle was a WAD, which is short for a weapon of ass destruction. Mom told us when we misbehaved, she would give us three swats with the paddle. "Not because I want to; it's because I love you."

After each WAD deployment, she wrote our name on the paddle along with the date. The paddle spent most of its days hanging on a nail on our kitchen wall by our refrigerator. Sometimes when we mis-behaved, she would simply point at the paddle. No words necessary. That was all it took for my sister. Not for me. Let's just say my name was on the paddle a lot more than Carmen's.

3

I don't know how long I was in my room. When she called for me to come upstairs, I pretended I couldn't hear. That made her yell louder.

"Caaarlosss, come upstairs."

I walked as slowly as I could, making my way out of my room and heading toward the stairs.

After Grandma died, I didn't like staying downstairs in my room. It felt weird sleeping down the hall from where she had died. One time I ran by her room toward mine and saw her sitting on her sofa. Her room was still the same, White Jesus and all. I slowed a bit, but then ran faster and slammed my door. After that I always ran by her room as fast as I could. I found reasons to sleep upstairs in my sister's room or I would sneak up and fall asleep on the couch. If I did have to stay in my room, I put a chair under the doorknob like in the movies. I know my grandma would never have hurt me, but I watched a lot of horror movies, and I wasn't willing to take any chances. I thought, *What if it's not Grandma and it's a vampire or a demon trying to get me?*

No evil creatures today, though, just my mom waiting for me upstairs. She called for me again. I was halfway up the stairs now. I remained silent. When I got to the top of the stairs, she was sitting at the dining room table where my grandma had taught me checkers. I assumed the position by lying on her lap, face down, cheeks up.

She said, "No. Sit down."

Okay? This was different. I sat down at the head of the table. I was wearing shorts. With every little adjustment my thighs peeled free and then reattached to the chair. My mom was holding a small white teacup instead of the paddle. This was all so confusing. I looked past my mom and into the kitchen. The paddle was hanging on the wall.

Next my mom placed the teacup on the table in front of me. It was one of her good ones that we were not allowed to use or touch.

"I want you to break this teacup."

I heard what she said, but none of what she was saying made sense to me. I looked at the cup and then back at her.

She said, "Break it."

"You want me to break it?"

"Yes. Break it."

"How? I don't know what—"

"Break the cup!"

Her eyes were wide with surprise. I don't think she meant to yell at me. It wasn't like her to lose control like that. She quickly calmed herself and said in a low voice, "Smash. The. Teacup. On. The. Table."

She was using what I called the "mom voice." The only thing I feared more than the "mom voice" was when it was accompanied by the "mom squeeze." This was usually applied to the back of my neck or around one of my triceps when we were in public. Enough pressure to know I was in for it, but not enough to leave a mark.

I picked up the little teacup with my right hand and raised it over my head. I held it there. She nodded. I then slammed that teacup on that table as hard as I could. It exploded into thousands of white shards.

Well, it seemed that way to me, but was probably only twelve or thirteen big pieces, and maybe thirty to forty tiny little pieces. They were all over the table and on the floor.

I looked at the table and the mess I had made. Then I saw it. *Shit.*

The cup had left a mark on the table. I looked at the mark and then at my mom. She then placed a bottle of Elmer's glue on the table. "Now I want you to put it back together."

She brushed away some of the pieces and then rubbed the mark with her thumb. It was more of a gouge and it didn't go away.

I gathered the pieces and began to put the teacup back together. My mom left me alone. I spent about thirty minutes trying to glue the teacup back together. When I was finished, I called her over. She inspected my work and said, "Is that cup the same as it was before?"

Fuck no, lady, that is not the same cup. Pieces were missing, and the ones that were connected by the glue were not where they had been before. This was a different teacup.

"No."

"Why?"

"Because . . . I broke it?"

"Mijo, trust is like a teacup. You broke my trust, just like you broke this teacup."

I looked down at my hands and began to peel the dried glue from my fingers.

"Mijo." I looked back at her. "It will never be the same." I looked back down at my hands. "Mijo, look at me."

I met her eyes.

"You broke my trust, but that doesn't mean I will never trust you again. If you want me to trust you again, we have to put it back together, piece by piece."

She gave me a hug and sent me to my room.

TEN

WHAT TASK FORCE?

1

I leaned over and whispered to Lieutenant Mead, "Ron, we can do this, or a version of it."

He nodded and gave me his "I know that; shut up and let me finish listening to this presentation" face.

We were at an anti–human trafficking conference in Washington, DC, listening to a cop from Florida present on proactive undercover operations. This was on a cold November day in 2014.

The cop explained how his task force would pose as teenagers and arrange for dates with men that wanted to have sex with teenagers. This would remind many people of the show *To Catch a Predator*, except there were no reporters here. The problem with that show was a reporter was interviewing the suspects, not a detective. Nowadays it's social media influencers who are setting up the predators. Then it was to get ratings, and now it's to get likes and follows. The problem with this is it does not hold people accountable for their actions.

I first met Ron when I was at WestNET. Ron always smiles unless you give him a reason not to. He takes care of his people. If Ron likes you, you know it. If Ron dislikes you, you know it. He speaks his mind. I respect people like that; there are no surprises that way.

When Ron gets angry, he turns Pizza Hut red—his face mostly, sometimes his neck. Because of this, he was given the nickname Red Ron before I met him. I experienced Red Ron several times. Thankfully it wasn't because of anything I did.

2

Later that evening Ron and I went to a local Irish pub for a few beers. We started to talk about MECTF and the presentation from earlier.

I said, "Ron, MECTF isn't a real task force. Not really. I have two guys, no admin support, and our area of responsibility is the entire state."

I was frustrated. Ron took a sip from his Guinness and kept listening to me.

I continued, "When I was at WestNET I had a real task force. Call MECTF what you want, but don't call it a task force."

Considering the cases we investigated involved protecting children and dealing with some of the darkest subject matter imaginable, I felt we should have more support.

On top of that, our task force had the unique ability to receive public and private grants as well as gifts to support the work of the task force. Of course, there were rules as to how the funds could be used. It puzzled me that before me nobody had utilized this revenue stream to its full potential. If someone did want to donate, they had to write a check or give cash. There was no mechanism in place to accept donations digitally.

I worked to change this. Citizens could pay for their vehicle registration online, so why couldn't we accept donations to protect children online? I spoke with an administrator in the WSP Budget and Fiscal Services about creating a way to accept the funds digitally.

"Thank you for taking the time to learn about my task force and helping me with setting up a way to accept funds to support our mission," I said.

She sounded bothered. "Well, it's a difficult process."

She must not have heard anything I'd said. My brow tightened as I clenched my teeth. "I'm sure it is. Thank you for taking the time to help me with this. I'm willing to do what it takes to make it happen."

"Like I said, it is a difficult process. I don't think this will be approved."

Okay, now I was bothered. "I see." I could hear my mom's voice: "Mijo, you control your emotions. Don't let her control you."

I paused and then answered the woman on the phone, "Well, I am willing to go through the difficult process if it means I can get the resources necessary to keep kids from being raped." I knew that was too far, but I kept going. "That's what we are talking about here. Stopping little kids from being raped. Are you willing to help me keep little kids from being raped?"

Silence. Yeah, I had crossed the line.

"Hello?"

"I am still here, Sergeant. I will get back to you."

I hung up the phone and thought, *No way this lady has kids.*

She did not get back to me. After a few weeks I went to the next person.

Lieutenant Ron used to tell me with a perma-grin pasted on his face, "I appreciate you Carlos, I do, but I need you to appreciate what I am about to tell you. Not everyone moves at Carlos speed, okay?"

"Well, they need to. This is bigger than all of us."

We were both right, but that didn't fix the problem. I needed to find a way to shift the priorities of my agency.

It took about two years, but I eventually got my way. The task force was finally able to accept donations through the WSP website. Two years to get this done is not "Carlos speed," but at least it got done.

3

Ron was good about letting me vent. He knew the way we were doing things was not sustainable.

This work takes so much from a person. When people asked me about the job, I used to say, "There is more cream than there is sour milk."

To me, the reward of removing kids from harm outweighed the negative impact on me. That's what I told myself. I mean, how could I say no to helping a kid? I didn't know how. I'm not built that way.

After a few beers, Ron and I talked about the anti–human trafficking conference presentation. He wanted us to do what he called a "Backpage case." At the time, Backpage was the leading online marketplace for commercial sex. Operating in ninety-seven countries and 943 locations worldwide and last valued at more than a half-billion dollars, Backpage was the world's second-largest classified advertising website. "Backpage [was] involved in 73% of all child trafficking reports that the National Center for Missing and Exploited Children (NCMEC) [received] from the general public (excluding reports by Backpage itself). The National Association of Attorneys General aptly described Backpage as a 'hub' of 'human trafficking, especially the trafficking of minors.'"[2] Backpage was seized by the Department of Justice in 2018 and no longer exists.

I told Ron, "I think we should do something similar to what we saw today, but not until we have the appropriate training."

He chimed back, "If city officers that aren't even in a task force can do Backpage cases, then why can't we!"

"I get it, but we need the appropriate training. I can give you a Backpage case, but it won't be the best case without the appropriate training. Get me the training."

4

When I was about eight years old, I was playing with my friend named Carl on the Fourth of July. Carl's parents took us to a crowded park in Colorado to listen to a symphony play music and to watch the fireworks. Carl's dad was a local cop, so my parents didn't mind when I went places with his family.

I remember running away with Carl from the crowd that was watching the symphony. We were two kids goofing around like kids do at that age. Carl and I found this little creek that was about one to two feet wide. We jumped back and forth over the creek, laughing the whole time.

Carl was a heavyset kid, so he was slower than me. He didn't have the best balance either. Every time after he jumped over the creek, he threw his arms out for balance. Most of his jumps resulted in him putting one of his hands down to keep from eating shit. Once he regained his balance, he would push his glasses back up onto his nose.

---

2   Rob Portman and Clair McCaskill, "Backpackage.com's Knowing Facilitation of Online Sex Trafficking," United States Senate, Permanent Subcommitte on Investigations, January 2017, https://www.courthousenews.com/wp-content/uploads/2017/02/Backpage-Report.pdf.

After a while, I noticed a man standing across from us on the other side of the creek. His pace was gradual, but I noticed him moving closer. A few minutes later he was directly across from us. I looked at Carl; he noticed the man too. We didn't have to say anything to each other; we both knew to stay on the opposite side of the creek from the man. There were a couple of sticks on the ground. We picked them up and poked them in and out of the creek trying to turn over some rocks.

The man wore a dark T-shirt and light gray sweatpants. His hands were in his pockets. The guy was fixated on us. He stood across from us and smiled like he had a secret he wanted to tell us. After a few minutes he couldn't help himself. "Hey, can I ask you boys a question?"

Carl and I looked at each other and didn't really think anything of it. I said, "Sure."

"Do you boys like girls?"

Carl and I both laughed a little. I said, "Yeah."

The smiling man said, "Do you like naked girls?" The smiling man was rolling something in one of his pockets, like a roll of quarters or something.

I said, "I don't know."

He said, "You can tell me if you do. I won't tell anybody. Have you ever seen a naked girl?"

We didn't answer him. We weren't laughing anymore.

The smiling man said, "I have some books in my van over there. They have naked girls in 'em."

We said nothing. Carl looked scared and I felt like Carl looked. The smiling man was only four to five feet away from us. I figured it would be easy enough for him to grab one of us. My grip tightened on my stick in case the smiling man tried anything. I looked at his hand again, the one rolling the quarters. I then felt sick when I realized it wasn't a roll of quarters in his pants. He was playing with himself. I quickly looked up at his face. His smile was bigger now, but he showed no teeth. He liked that I'd noticed he was touching himself. That's when I heard the symphony. It started to play the theme song to *Raiders of the Lost Ark.* I don't know why, but I was energized.

I looked at Carl and yelled, "It's *Raiders of the Lost Ark*! Let's go!"

Carl and I ran as fast as if we were Indy running from the natives. Although Carl was built like Eric Cartman from *South Park*, I was having a hard time keeping up with him. I never saw a fat kid run so fast.

We couldn't find his dad, but we did find three police officers. They were standing together talking about who knows what.

We stopped about five feet from them. After the run, Carl looked like someone had sprayed him with a hose. His hair was sticking to his forehead, and he was bent over with his hands on his thighs, gasping for air. He waved one arm to me and said, "You, you tell 'em."

"No man, you do it. They probably know your dad."

He could barely get the words out, "Just do it!"

I walked over to the officers. One saw me and nodded to his partners. "Can I help you, son?"

I didn't know what to say exactly. I blurted out, "Um, yeah, we saw a butt-raper guy." The officers tried not to laugh, but they all did. I continued, "I mean, the guy tried to show us pictures of naked ladies and get us to his van. He was touching his, um, thing. His penis. In his pants." Shit, I felt stupid.

The smiles fell off their faces. They asked me to show them where it had happened and which way the smiling man had gone. Carl and I ran in the direction where we had last seen the man. This time I was in the lead and Carl was struggling to keep up. While we ran, I could hear the officers talking on their radios. We showed them where we'd last seen the smiling man. The sticks were there, but no man. He was gone.

5

I was an eight-year-old kid with no idea of what a sex trafficker looked like. My parents had never talked to me about stranger danger. I was clueless. Even so, Carl and I both knew the smiling man was a creep.

While at MECTF, all the cases I worked involved sex crimes against children. I learned quickly the kids being raped in the series of photos and videos I saw were not just from other countries. They were kids that lived in the United States. They lived in my own state. Some of them attended the same schools that my kids attended.

The cases rarely involved some creepy guy in a white van snatching kids off the street or, in my case, from a park. Most kids are smart enough to stay away from those guys.

The offenders and traffickers I usually encountered were family members or someone close to the child. Sometimes it was a child running away from abuse at home and then selling themselves to survive.

I thought if my team worked proactively, we could remove some kids from harm and focus on the demand. What I mean by focus on the demand is go after the persons seeking to have sex with children whether they paid for the sex or not. Think of it this way. You are the owner of a cookie store. If people quit buying your cookies, you will go out of business. That's what we wanted to do: Close the store.

I wanted my detectives to receive additional training for multiple reasons. First off, we didn't know everything. Second, I needed my team to be mentally prepared for what we were about to embark on.

I also knew that once we made arrests, we might have to testify in criminal trials. This meant being attacked by a defense attorney or a defense team. If we didn't have the appropriate training, their attacks would most likely be successful. What was at stake was too important to simply run a quick operation to snag a headline. Ron agreed and helped us get the training we needed.

6

A few days later we traveled back to Washington state. Ron went to work. The first thing he did was secure funds to send one detective and myself to a specialized interview course. The course focused on interviewing persons that were sexually attracted to children. It took a year, but in 2014 Ron set aside the funds for us to take the course.

The training technique we learned at that course was created by Dr. Joe Sullivan at Forensic Solutions. The goal of the technique is to provide a comprehensive insight into understanding the behavior of perpetrators of sex crimes against children. The interview system is specifically designed to enhance the skills and knowledge base of professionals who interview child sex offenders. The training was supposed to help me quickly assess the person sitting in front of me and get him from "I didn't do it" to "Yes I did, and this is how."

Ron was eventually promoted to captain and left our division. I was happy for him, but sad for me.

My command staff came and went, but most said the same things: "Great job." "I'm glad you are doing this because I couldn't do it." "We have your back." "Let me know what you need." That was the worst one: "Let me know what you need." What I needed were bodies. I needed detectives and equipment to do my job. I didn't need lip service.

Shortly after Ron was promoted to captain, his replacement told me I was receiving the Chief's Award for Professional Excellence. This award is given to employees who perform specific or sustained acts of outstanding service. It generally recognizes distinct instances of high-level performance.

I asked, "What's this for?"

"Los, really? It's for what you have done with MECTF."

I said, "I don't want this. This belongs to the team, not me."

While I was talking with the lieutenant, our captain was nearby, and he heard what we were talking about. He said, "Los, you are the leader. Your team is successful because of your efforts. You are getting the award."

I went to the award ceremony and accepted the award and was given a chief's coin. A chief's coin is what it sounds like—a metal coin that the chief of the WSP gives to people as a token of their thanks. I took the opportunity to tell those that attended the ceremony about my task force and how this award was theirs. I was accepting the award and coin on behalf of my team.

Don't get me wrong, I was thankful for the recognition, but I wanted more than a piece of etched tin glued to a shiny piece of wood.

After the ceremony I thanked my captain. I held up the coin, shaking it back and forth, and said, "So how does this work?"

He said, "How does what work?"

"The reward program. After I collect three of these do I trade them in for a detective?"

He pushed his head back, pressing his lips together. He was not amused. Before he could answer, I held out my hand to shake his and said, "Thank you, sir."

My command staff had nominated me for the award because they were proud of what I had done with the task force and our community. I admit, it does feel good to be recognized, but I felt guilty.

I hadn't done any of it on my own. We were a team. It was always a team effort. I felt if they wanted to recognize "my" work, then we should all be recognized. I also felt if they really wanted to reward me, they needed to get me resources.

E L E V E N

GI JOE

CONTENT WARNING

As noted on the copyright page, while adults should be free to review any of this material and may find it to be informative, reader discretion is advised. This chapter contains content about criminal sexual activities involving children that may be offensive to some adults and is inappropriate for minors.

1

It was early February 2014, and my phone was ringing. I got a lot of phone calls. It was FBI Special Agent Ted Bennett. Ted was assigned to the FBI's South Sound Child Exploitation Task Force (SSCETF) in Tacoma, Washington. We were both short on resources, so it made sense for us to work cases together.

Ted is a wee fella like me. Ya know, we are both as tall as a grown man's chest. The main difference is Ted is built like a brick house. The dude is jacked. Ted cusses like Owen Wilson. He doesn't use the fun words like *fuck*, *shit*, or *damn* . He prefers *wow*, *jeepers*, and *really*.

I remember one time asking him, "I interviewed this guy

yesterday. He asked me a question and I didn't know the answer. It's really been bothering me. I was thinking, maybe you might know the answer."

He said, "Anything to help, man."

I paused briefly, then said, "He asked me why the FBI's badge is so small. Ted, I don't know why. I panicked, so I told the guy it was to reduce the federal deficit. He seemed happy with that, but I feel empty inside not knowing the truth." I tried to maintain a straight face, but the laughs spoiled my delivery.

Ted smiled and said, "Wow."

"Yeah, I know. Thing is, I really workshopped this one, and that can't be the reason. As you know, all the other federal agencies have larger badges than yours."

"Really, Los?"

"Ted, it's a valid question."

2

Ted wasn't calling me with the answer. This was a call for help. Florida law enforcement had contacted the FBI and now Ted was calling me.

A little girl in Florida had disclosed that her stepdad had tied her up and raped her multiple times. She detailed how the stepdad had photographed, filmed, and streamed the sex acts online. The stepdad was an active-duty army soldier stationed at JBLM.

When I first started at MECTF, a call like this required me to take a minute to get my bearings. It's like experiencing tremors from a small quake but not realizing it's a quake until it's finished. Not this time. This was second nature now.

Did the call upset me? Yes. If it didn't upset me then it meant it was time for me to stop doing this work. At least that's what I would tell myself.

Did I have time to dwell on it? No.

We learned the soldier, GI Joe or Joe for short, lived in an apartment complex in Spanaway, Washington, which is near JBLM. We didn't know whether Joe was on base or at home. We did know Joe was supposed to meet with his command staff for an unrelated matter.

Our plan was to send two detectives to JBLM to interview GI Joe. The interview would take place on JBLM at the Criminal Investigations Division (CID) headquarters. We hoped to get Joe while he was on the base. The rest of the team would then serve a search warrant at his residence to look for evidence supporting the allegations.

When we set up on a location or area, we called it "setting the box." Imagine a place or an area that you want to watch. Now draw a box around it. The idea is to know what goes in and out of the box. Once the box was set, we started on a search warrant affidavit. I had some detectives set the box at Joe's apartment. A few hours later we had a warrant for his apartment.

My fear was Joe had destroyed evidence already. We knew the little girl had told her grandmother what Joe did to her. The grandmother, Joe's mother, told Joe what the little girl had said. This increased the chance that whatever we were searching for might not be there.

Working these cases, I knew even if Joe deleted things from his computer, there could still be traces left. Sometimes it was great evidence, and other times we were fucked. There was always a chance we wouldn't find anything.

I decided to do the interview with another detective. I didn't think Joe was going to participate in the interview since he had been tipped off. I figured once he said no, we would join the rest of the team at the search warrant site.

Even though I doubted Joe would speak with me, I wanted him to. I was excited, but more nervous than usual. I was nervous because this was the first time I would get to apply the new interviewing technique I had learned at my Forensic Solutions training.

3

A few CID agents contacted Joe and were transporting him to their headquarters. We waited there for Joe in a medium-sized interview room.

The room was nothing special—four plain beige walls with a medium-sized rectangular table in the center with two chairs tucked neatly on each side. I pushed the table against the wall farthest from the entrance to the room and placed one of the chairs in the center of the room. That would be Joe's chair. I placed the other chair closer to the table; that was my chair. I didn't want any barriers between us. Another chair was added for Luke, one of my detectives.

Luke and I worked narcotics together while in WestNET. I recruited him to work child exploitation cases with me. Luke is Samoan.

Have you seen the meme of the Rock's head on Kevin Hart's body? That's Luke, but with hair, and Luke doesn't talk as much as Kevin Hart. Actually, Luke doesn't speak that much at all. When he does speak, his words are quiet and kind.

4

Luke never cussed, well not intentionally. But we had a case while in WestNET where the person's last name was spelled PHUCK. I watched Luke read the name. His eyes widened a bit. "Hey Sarge, how would you say his last name?"

"Great question, Luke. I *do* believe it is pronounced FUCK."

Luke failed to hide his discomfort. He said softly, "Frick, man. You think so?"

When Luke said "frick," it always made me laugh. I mean, it's the same thing. The intent is the same. "Yes, Luke. FUCK. Come on, Luke, say it with me . . . FFFUUUCCKKK."

Luke hesitated and then quietly said, "Phuck."

Over the next few weeks, the team formulated questions to get Luke to say "Phuck" as much as possible.

When Phuck was arrested, Luke learned *Phuck* was pronounced FOOK and not FUCK.

I thought, *Well, it was fun while it lasted.*

Luke was wearing what I liked to call his Sunday best. I lived in Oklahoma for seven years, which is also known as a part of the Bible Belt. From my experience, most people in the town I lived in either went to church, got in trouble, or did both. I did both. Anyway, Sunday best was what everybody wore to church, and Luke dressed that way every day—a dress shirt and tie with a pullover V-neck sweater along with slacks and polished dress shoes.

A few minutes later, CID brought Joe into the room. He had black sweatpants on, and a long-sleeved heather-gray T-shirt clung tightly to his surprisingly large belly. The word *ARMY* stretched across his chest. His head had been buzzed short with what looked like a size 1 clipper guard. Joe sat down in the center of the room.

Joe wasn't what I expected. He had what I call "moobs," or man boobs. They rested on his belly, and his belly sat on his lap.

No way this guy passed his PT. GI Joe looked like shit.

5

Luke and I introduced ourselves.

I told Joe why we were there and that we wanted to talk to him about the incident with his stepdaughter, M. I asked him if that was okay. He flashed us an awkward smile and, to my surprise, he agreed to speak with us. I read Joe his rights and then began.

As per my training, I started with building a timeline. I asked Joe how he had grown up, where he had grown up, if he had any siblings, if his parents were still together, were they alive, and so on. My plan was to build off that. I wanted to know the events in his life all the way up to him sitting in the chair across from me.

Remember, this was the first time I'd used a timeline like this during an interview. Although I saw the value of it in the training course, I felt anxious. I wanted to just get to the point. I remember thinking, *This is stupid. This is a waste of time.* I wanted to get to the questions about what Joe had done. Instead, I stayed on target and began building the timeline.

When we talked about things that Joe believed had nothing to do with the case, his demeanor changed. His shoulders relaxed, and he stopped crossing his arms; instead, he used them to describe his life. At times he smiled; sometimes he laughed. Joe shared with us that both of his parents were still alive. He had two brothers and one sister. Joe told us he had married his wife because he thought his stepdaughter was his biological daughter. He learned later she was not. Joe shared how he had another child with his wife and how both kids were living with her in Florida.

Joe detailed how he'd moved from one city to the next. The longer we talked, the more comfortable he became with me. After getting to know him a little bit better, I asked him about his mother telling him about the allegations.

"What did you do once your mother called you?"

He said, "She told me she was getting a lawyer."

"What was your response?"

"I told her it's a lie. I've never done anything to her. It broke my heart. How could she say something like this, ya know?"

Joe paused. Then he apologized and scrunched his face as if he were about to cry. No tears fell. He had zero tears in his eyes. His chest raised and rested at the same pace as when we had been speaking earlier. Joe continued, "Sorry. I just . . . I did everything for them. I fought for seven years to get custody. I protect them from everything I possibly can protect them from."

I tend to fidget, especially when someone is feeding me bullshit. I focused on staying still in my chair. I said nothing. I listened.

"I mean, I do expect a lot from them, like ya know, before I buy them big-item things, like tablets . . . or phones. Like M's Nintendo DS. I made her wait. She had to show me she was responsible. Responsible enough to take care of something like that."

I said, "I got kids. I mean, they have to earn it. Especially in this day and age when everything is so easy."

Joe pretended to wipe more invisible tears from his eyes, then he poked his right eye with his thumb. *Nice try, Joe.*

I asked him, "What do you think should happen to someone who rapes a kid?"

Joe straightened up and quickly said, "You need to put them in jail or give them the death sentence."

His response sounded rehearsed. Still . . . no tears.

"Joe. Can I call you Joe?"

"Yes you can."

"Joe, we have the ability to find things. For instance, we can find things on computers even if they have been deleted. Things like photos and videos. I do it all the time. I can search for things that are uploaded to the internet."

I held up my hand and pointed to the pad of my index finger. "Everything that is placed on a computer or uploaded to the internet has a fingerprint. We search for those fingerprints."

Joe's chest began to rise and fall more quickly. He rubbed his hands on his sweatpants like he had just washed them but there were no paper towels to dry them off. Luke saw it too. He left the room.

I said, "Let's say we have a picture of you and somebody . . . and it is illegal. That picture has a fingerprint. In this example, we capture that fingerprint. We have software that searches devices and the internet for that fingerprint and locates it. We search for it. We retrieve it. Then we go get the person that created it. That is one of the things we do."

Luke came back with some water for Joe.

I could hear Joe breathing now. The pace was faster than before and with shorter intervals in between each breath.

"Would it surprise you that we located a photo of you with M that was illegal?"

He answered, "Yes, it would. I have never done anything like that."

In. Out. Faster. Shorter.

"Why do you think M said you raped her?"

"I don't know. She was mad at me for taking away her tablet."

"That is pretty extreme. It's a tablet."

Joe told us M's therapist supported him and was shocked that she would say this.

"Joe, we have a warrant for all your electronic data. We are at your apartment . . . right now. We are using that software to search for those images. This is happening as I sit here with you. I'm telling you this because I want to ask you a question."

"Okay."

I asked, "Is there anything there . . . at your house in Lakewood? If there is, we will find it."

He said, "No."

"Joe, our unit is a little bit different than others. I understand that you are a person. The people we get a chance to talk to are still people, even if they have done horrible things. People who do horrible things are still people."

"Okay."

"Joe, some of the allegations are that you tied her up."

"I never tied her up."

"You have never tied her up?"

"No."

"Do you have any ropes or restraints?"

"I have under-the-bed restraints that me and my ex-wife used to use, but I never tied her up."

I did not believe him. "What do those look like?"

He cupped his hands around his wrists and said, "They are just like, um, the ones that you put underneath the mattress. With, um, soft cuffs. That's it."

I said nothing and waited.

"They were underneath the bed already."

The silence swallowed his confidence. I sat still and watched him, waiting for him to speak.

"I never used them on her."

"Okay, I was just thinking about the cuffs. What's your fantasy, if you even have a fantasy?"

Joe smiled. "I did my fantasy with one of the girls I was seeing. It was a dominatrix kind of thing where she brought over her toys and I used them on her. We did what we did. That's my only fantasy."

"Did it start with you in control and then roles changed, or was it all you?"

Joe answered, "It was all me. I was in control the whole time. It was forceful."

"Did you ever do this at home or in a place where the kids could hear you or see what you were doing by accident?"

"No, the kids were always gone."

"Joe, did you ever catch M watching porn?"

"Yes."

"Was it similar to what you just described to me? Forceful. Dominatrix. Restraints?"

"It was normal."

Joe painted himself as being misunderstood and played the victim. I didn't buy it. Joe enjoyed being in control and hurting others.

"Joe, I am asking you these things because of what you are explaining to me: the fantasy and what you have done sexually. That is what M said is happening to her."

I wanted to confront him with the pain of what M had gone through and see if he was remorseful or if he was excited by the pain. "You . . . being in control. Her . . . wanting you to stop. You . . . telling her no. You doing what you want."

Joe showed no remorse. The only emotion he displayed was fear.

"That is what concerns me. The fantasy you just explained to me is what she is disclosing has happened. Do you see how that can be troublesome?"

Joe nodded. "Yeah."

"A ten-year-old should not know how to do that."

Again, he nodded. "Yeah."

"Let's draw this out."

I picked up a pen and wrote out the word "FANTASY" on a piece of paper.

"Here is a person's fantasy."

As I spoke, I wrote out the words describing his fantasy.

"It deals with bondage, tying up, and being in control."

I watched him study the words as I put them on the paper. He began to lick his lips. Joe was reliving it. He was there, in the moment with her.

I continued, "And then you have this little girl. This little ten-year-old girl that is saying this started happening to her when she was seven."

He nodded more slowly. "Mm-hmm."

"It's matching the fantasy. It's matching your fantasy. This is what she is saying her dad did, yet you are telling me she has not been exposed to that."

He continued to stare at the page.

"So how do you explain that? Me looking at it from the outside, it doesn't look good."

His eyes stayed on the paper as if him staring at it longer would make it change somehow.

"So what I am trying to get is the explanation of why this happened."

His hands gripped each other tightly, turning his fingers white. I could see his scalp turning red through his hair.

I continued, "If it did happen, which I believe it did, if you have some remorse for it, it would be good to show that instead of denying, denying, denying, because it makes you look like a monster."

I paused for a bit.

I struggle with letting the silence sit. It's hard not to fill the little gaps, those awkward spaces we have all experienced in a conversation, the ones we rush to fill so we feel better. From my training and experience, it's best to sit in that silence and let the other person fill that space. If you rush to fill it, you may miss something. If the person pauses for several minutes and doesn't fill the space, then you continue.

"From what I am seeing, you are someone that likes to be in control. You explained it. I have a little girl telling me that, but there is a reason behind everything. I believe that. There is a reason why you are this way. There is a reason why this happened. I want to know why."

Joe was nodding with me as I talked.

"If you continue to tell me that it didn't happen when everything is telling me it did happen, then we might as well put your face up on that wall with the word 'MONSTER' over it," I said, pointing at the bare wall.

Joe looked down at his hands in his lap. He stopped squeezing them. His white fingers were now turning pink.

"I don't think you are a monster, Joe."

I lied. Joe is a monster. I asked, "Do you need help?"

He whispered, "Yes."

"Then I need you to tell me, Joe. Tell me what you did."

Joe started to cry. For real this time. "I don't want to go to jail."

That was a true statement. Joe wasn't crying because he was ashamed for what he had done to M. He was crying because he knew he had been caught. He knew he was going to jail and he didn't want that.

We continued our conversation, and we talked about the horrific things he did to that little girl—things that I will not describe in detail in this book or probably ever.

Joe admitted he had raped M at least fifteen times in a string of assaults spanning three years, strapping her to a bed during several of the attacks. He admitted to streaming the rapes via Skype so others could watch. On one occasion he had viewers instruct him on what to do to her.

A few days after I met Joe, I helped transport him from the county jail to the federal detention center. I followed behind Joe and an FBI agent as they walked down a dimly lit hallway. I can still hear the sound of his metal restraints echoing down that hallway as he slowly shuffled toward his new life.

The monster was sentenced to twenty-five years in the federal system.

Yes, this is a good sentence, but I feel it is too short considering the long-term impact of his conduct. Let's just say if I were Zeus, Joe would be cast into Tartarus, the deepest, darkest pit in the underworld, to be tormented and suffer for his wicked acts for all eternity.

6

Cases like this supported the reasons why we needed to work with the SSCETF. In the spring of 2014 MECTF moved from Olympia, Washington, to Tacoma, Washington, where we were colocated with the SSCETF. It just made sense, but one thing I didn't plan on was how the move would impact my wellness routine.

To help my detectives separate their work from their family lives, I had a few rules. I didn't allow them to view any images or any other graphic material during the last two hours of their shifts. I call that material the Ugly.

If a prosecutor gave us a deadline and we needed to view the Ugly later in the day, then I approved overtime for them so they could separate from the Ugly before they went home.

Answer this question: How many times have you gone home and told your family, "I need fifteen minutes"? Fifteen minutes to get yourself settled. Now answer this question: How many times did you get your fifteen minutes?

The thing is, your family is excited to see you. They want to know about your day and tell you about theirs. That last two hours is important. It helps create a barrier between you and the Ugly by focusing on something other than the Ugly. It sets the stage for you to be present with those who love you.

My separation routine was to drive about forty-five minutes to an hour to a Starbucks that was on my way home. I would get my iced tea and park behind a local steak house in a mostly empty parking lot. I would play Clash of Clans on my iPhone and then drive home. When I got home, I was ready to be present with my family.

When MECTF moved to Tacoma, it messed up my routine. I didn't realize it until a few days after the change.

One day Julie asked me, "What's wrong? Why have you been so angry lately?"

I wasn't following my own advice. I was taking the Ugly home. After Julie talked to me, I thought about it for a bit and realized it was my routine. I needed to fix this. I found a new Starbucks and made my adjustment. The change helped me to decompress before I got home, and I was less angry. Things were better for us. I was better to be around because I was present.

I want to tell you the adjustment was permanent, that my new routine was permanent, but it wasn't. After a few weeks I went off-track. I wasn't consistent, and it weighed on me. If I could go back, I would tell my younger self to make the time. Make the adjustment. It only takes thirty minutes to an hour.

If you do this work, take the time for yourself so you are better for those around you. So you are better for yourself. So you are better for the mission.

TWELVE

NET NANNY

1

To get to Ron's Backpage case, I wanted us to be trained as undercover chatters. We were approved to attend the ICAC chat and online investigations training. Although Ron was no longer with our task force, his support helped build the foundation to what would become a series of operations called Operation Net Nanny.

Side note: I never liked the name Net Nanny. I was asked to come up with a name for the operation a few days before the first one and I thought, *We take care of kids on the internet, it's like we are babysitters. Net Nanny.*

I tried to change the name for future operations, but people kept referring to it as Net Nanny, so I was stuck with it. We just added a number to the end after each operation. I don't know why cops like to name the operations, but they do. I guess people think it's cool. Too bad I picked such a lame name.

2

Our goal during these operations was to proactively target persons seeking to sexually abuse kids. The concept of the operation was simple. We would communicate online posing as adults or at-risk youth. We had several different personas.

For the adult personas, we posed as adults that controlled kids aged thirteen and younger that were available for sex. We also posed as adults seeking to have sex with kids. The at-risk youth were usually between the ages of twelve and thirteen.

We picked thirteen and younger for several reasons. First, these were the ages we dealt with in our cases. Second, the state laws in this range come with stiff penalties. Someone that attempts to rape a child aged twelve to thirteen years old in Washington state is looking at five years to life. If someone attempts to rape a child that is eleven years old or younger, they are facing ten years to life.

Remember, my task force was small with limited resources, so this effort was a no-brainer for me. I made the decision to focus on the most egregious crimes that came with the stiffest penalties.

I broke operations down into four sections: triage, contact, arrest, and follow-up.

1. Triage: This is where we triage the responses to our undercover (UC) profiles. This was done by me or those that I had assigned to chat as a UC. We focused on those wanting to exploit children. Let's refer to them as the target or targets. During this part of the operation, we gathered evidence and intelligence on our targets. This helped give us an idea as to who was showing up to meet us. It also helped identify children they may have offended upon before we met them.

2. Contact: Once the target agreed to meet with the UC, we sent

the target to a location predetermined by me. We liked to use convenience stores because they are easy for a surveillance team to blend in. Before the target arrived at that location, our surveillance team would be set up in the area. Once the target was identified, we would move the target to a new predetermined location where, if all went as planned, they would be arrested.

3. Arrest: The surveillance team followed the target to the next location, where they were handed off to a perimeter team and/ or an arrest team. This varied depending on the scenario and any safety concerns we may have identified. The target was contacted and arrested.

CONCEPT OF OPERATION

Properly trained and commissioned investigators communicate online in an undercover capacity identifying those wanting to exploit children or traffic vulnerable persons. These investigators develop Probable Cause (PC) for the case.

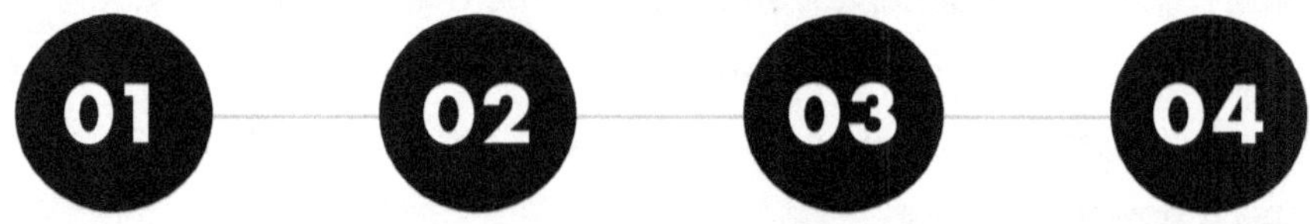

TRIAGE

Triage the responses to UC profiles. Focus on child exploitation and human trafficking cases. Gather evidence and intelligence to prepare for future contact/potential arrest/identification of live victims.

CONTACT

Arrange for a meeting at a predetermined location. This is where surveillance identifies your target and surveils them to another location. Once identified, the UC chatter will provide the next location to the target.

ARREST

Surveillance stays with the target until the hand-off is made to the perimeter team/arrest team. This varies depending on the location, the availability of the UC, and safety concerns.

FOLLOW-UP

Work to identify live victims and conduct the appropriate follow-up for the victims and the case. This includes good interviews, a good intel analyst, working with service providers, knock and talks, etc.

Graphic by Carlos Rodriguez

4. Follow-up: After the arrest, the real work started. We worked to identify live victims and conduct the appropriate follow-up necessary for a solid case. This included interviewing the suspect, digital forensic analysis, procuring search warrants, providing services for victims, and documenting all our work in a case file.

We focused online in areas where we knew this activity was taking place. Now you may be thinking, *Where does this activity happen?*

Some of you may think this only happens on the darknet, at the border, or with sick people who are members of some secret "Eyes Wide Shut" society. Well, it does not.

Most of the cases from these operations were listed on Craigslist in their Casual Encounters section and on popular social media applications.

Craigslist is a website for viewing and posting local advertisements. It works a lot like the classifieds section of a newspaper, and it's completely free to use. You can find a listing for almost anything on Craigslist, such as jobs, apartments, garage sales, used cars, and a whole lot more.

You can easily connect with people near you to find, buy, or sell just about anything. Including sex with children.

This happens everywhere.

Ordering a child for sex is as easy as ordering a pizza. Make no mistake. It happens everywhere, including where you live.

3

Although the concept was simple, implementing it was not. It isn't easy to play the part of someone wanting to purchase kids for sex. It is even more difficult to play the part of someone offering up children for sex, especially if it's their own kids.

After being trained to interview persons that were sexually attracted to kids, I visited Morgan in prison—not because she was my friend, but because I wanted to understand more about her and her thought process. I wanted feedback from our interview with her to improve our interview process. I wanted to know why she felt so comfortable talking with Jeff.

I learned that explaining the interview process is extremely important. The first time I met with Morgan in prison, she told me she didn't like me. I was shocked and didn't understand why. I didn't remember speaking to her during the interview, so why did she dislike me?

Morgan pointed at me and said, "You, you just sat there and judged me. You didn't say anything."

I apologized to her and explained that when we conducted interviews, we used two people. One person was designated as the lead in the interview. We called them the one; in her case that was Jeff. My role was to support him, and I would speak up if Jeff had missed something. We called the support interviewer the two.

Morgan responded, "You should have told me that. I can't read your mind. When you interview the next person, explain what you are doing. It will help them relax."

Morgan helped me become a better interviewer. She also shared more about her upbringing and what she had been through as a child. This helped me build an undercover persona that I used to talk with what ended up being hundreds of people wanting to rape children.

4

After our first operation, we were requested to conduct one in Tacoma, Washington. After that operation we were asked to conduct one in Snohomish County, which is north of Seattle. The requests kept coming in and we kept scheduling operations.

Given all the requests, I decided to meet with my command staff and suggested we should travel around the state conducting these operations. I wanted to show this happened in every WSP district.

The WSP breaks up the state into different areas of responsibility called districts. Washington state has eight main districts, each with its own Criminal Investigations Unit led by a detective sergeant with several detectives and an administrative assistant assigned to them. The WSP also has several drug task forces and several auto-theft task forces throughout the state.

Then there was the MECTF. The WSP had one MECTF, which was understaffed. Our area of responsibility was the entire state. We were expected to provide direct assistance and case management, technical assistance, and personnel training across the state. This included assisting other police agencies.

Think about that for a minute. How was my small task force supposed to address the following issues?

- Child sex trafficking

- Possession/manufacture/distribution of CSAM

- Enticement of our children

- Child rape

- Child molestation

In my mind the solution was simple: more resources. I wanted an MECTF in every district, not just one for the entire state.

Now I had to figure out how to make that happen. I needed to show our value so my agency would make a shift in its priorities. Not all resources are free. We also needed funding from the state legislature.

I knew crimes against children were a problem across the state, so I wanted to conduct these operations around the state to identify the areas where it was more prevalent. This would also give me the data my agency needed to draft a legislative action request (LAR) asking for additional funds to support MECTF appropriately.

My command staff agreed with me. The next step was to make friends. We partnered with law enforcement around the state and conducted these undercover stings across the state.

In the beginning I was so nervous. I worried nobody was going to show and it would be a waste of everyone's time. I was so wrong.

Before I left MECTF, my agency sent forward two LARs. Although I didn't get an MECTF in every district, the WSP did receive funds to add additional detectives, training, equipment, and support. They added an Eastside MECTF, but for me it still wasn't enough. It still isn't enough.

THIRTEEN

THE WOLF

> **CONTENT WARNING**
>
> As noted on the copyright page, while adults should be free to review any of this material and may find it to be informative, reader discretion is advised. This chapter contains content about criminal sexual activities involving children that may be offensive to some adults and is inappropriate for minors.

1

It was the summer of 2016. I was driving to interview a thirty-year-old man we had arrested the day before. If I remember it correctly, this was our fifth Net Nanny operation. We were in the middle of the operation, and the man I was headed to interview had been arrested for attempting to rape an eleven-year-old girl. I always called this guy the Wolf for two reasons: His name sounded like the word *wolf*, and he was a wolf in sheep's clothing.

During his interview with detectives, he denied ever having had sex with minors, but he did admit to viewing and trading CSAM. The Wolf agreed to take a polygraph, and the results indicated he was deceptive regarding offending on children. When the prosecutor learned the results, she asked me to interview the man at the jail before his arraignment. This was the first time I had ever gone to the jail to interview a suspect after they had been interviewed. I thought, *No way is this guy going to talk with me.*

Since we were in the middle of an operation, a lot was going on. The timing was not ideal, but it didn't matter; the prosecutor wanted to give it a shot, so I moved things around to make it happen. Plus, I didn't think I would be there that long and I could grab another Starbucks iced tea.

During this operation we had a young trooper cross-training with the task force. I brought him with me as my number two for the interview. We all called him the Kid.

2

When I first met the Kid, I was shocked that someone looked younger than me when I first started. He looked so young that we used the Kid as one of our undercover teen decoys.

The Kid had fine sandy-blond hair and a permanent smile. His skin was so pale, his rosy cheeks looked like they were painted on his face. I didn't know it at the time, but the Kid had had a difficult life before joining the WSP.

The Kid's mom had raised him and his brother by herself. He helped his mom take care of his younger brother the best he knew how. He didn't have the luxury of being only a brother; he was a care-taker, a parent, and oftentimes a protector. The Kid made the decision to help others instead of being consumed by the pain and hardships from his life. You see, he didn't want what happened to him or his family to happen to anybody else, just like I didn't want others to go through the pain that Julie's family had gone through when her brother David died. So he chose to become a state trooper and protect others in addition to his own family. To this day, the Kid fights injustice the best he knows how. When we bump into each other, he still gives me that smile.

3

We sat in my car for a few minutes.

I said, "I will ask most of the questions."

He said, "Yes, Sarge."

"Our goal is to identify any live victims and have him tell us what he did."

"Yes, Sarge."

"If you need a break because of what he says, it's okay. Just tell me, and we can take a break or you can step out. It depends on the flow."

"Okay, Sarge."

"I mean it."

"Copy, Sarge."

The Kid had never been a part of an interview like this. I was worried for him. I wasn't sure how he would respond to what the Wolf said, like it might fuck him up mentally. I was also worried the Kid might fuck up my interview. I didn't know what he was made of yet.

4

Jails have their own unique odor. Most smell like a sweaty man that shit himself in a bathroom and all he could find to cover the smell was a bottle of Pine-Sol.

We spoke with the corrections officer at intake; she provided us with a room to interview the Wolf. The room was made up of painted off-white cinder blocks. It contained three plastic chairs and a small white table. We remained standing as we waited for them to bring us the Wolf.

I said, "Hey, don't smile so much. At least not until we see how this goes. I don't want him to think you are laughing at him."

The smile left his face. "Okay, Sarge."

He looked weird without the smile; now I could see how nervous he was.

"Okay, smile a little bit."

The door opened. A corrections officer walked in and pointed at the chair across from us. A small-framed man sat down in the chair. He was wearing an orange jumpsuit, and his shaggy auburn hair fell slightly over his glasses. He wasn't menacing at all. His arms were the same width from his wrists all the way up to his arm-pits. I thought if this guy fell out of his chair, he would break. His hands were cuffed in front of him. We introduced ourselves and sat down across from him at the table. We advised him of his rights and began.

5

Before I interview someone, my heart flutters and I get lightheaded, like when you get up too quickly. It's my nerves, they get at me. Every time.

They get at me because the outcome of the conversation I am about to have can determine whether someone is held accountable for harming a child or not. More importantly, it can prevent someone from ever doing it again.

Sometimes my left eyelid twitches like a metronome of a thou-sand tiny electric zaps, one after the other. I raise my eyebrows a few times, making my eyes bigger to get rid of the zaps, but it doesn't really help. My chest tightens.

I have a routine to calm myself, like baseball star Ichiro Suzuki does on every trip to the plate. He takes a deep breath, holds his bat at arm's length, and tugs his right sleeve with his left hand.

First, I take a deep breath in through my nose, and my chest expands. I hold it for a few seconds and then slowly release it out through my mouth. Next, I spin my wrists in circles until they pop. I think, *Breathe. Settle. Focus.* A calmness takes hold of me, and then I am ready.

I don't plan out each question before I interview someone. I mean, I anticipate some of the questions and I have a preconceived idea of how the person may present themselves to me, but I never really know what the person is going to say or do.

Based on my training and experience, I know people present an image of who they want me to believe they are. Think of it like this: When you are with your family, you act differently than when you are with coworkers. We all present differently depending on our audience. It is no different when I interview someone. My biggest hope is they want to engage in a conversation with me.

Usually, I can tell early in the interview who they are choosing for me to see. I ask my questions based on how they present themselves to me and build from there. I use an empathetic approach and try to ask open-ended questions. This has served me well, but I don't always get it right.

I attempt to understand the person in front of me, which helps me stay focused on the task at hand and regulates me. It allows me to be present in the room with a person that chooses to harm children. It helps me stay in that room even when I don't feel like being there.

6

I can think of only two occasions where I needed to take a break during an interview. One time I was interviewing a man in his early twenties who wanted to have sex with two girls ages eleven and six years old. A forensic search was conducted on his cell phone, and we located sexually explicit images of what appeared to be a ten- to twelve-year-old little girl. I handed the questioning off to my partner and my mind started to race.

This is someone's son. I can't imagine what I would do if this was my boy. Oh, God! Don't think that! Noah could never. What happened to this guy to make him like this?

I don't remember what the suspect was saying, but I interrupted him to say, "I . . . I am having a hard time right now." I cleared my throat. Nothing was in it, but I felt a need to clear it. "I need to step outside for a minute."

My partner's eyes were wide with disbelief. He squinted them slightly and said, "Okay." He said okay, but his face asked if I was okay.

I nodded at my partner and stepped outside. It only took me about five minutes to eliminate the thoughts from my mind and reset. I drank some water and rejoined the interview.

The second time was much different. The man I was interviewing had shown up to rape a three-year-old baby. I wanted to wrap my hands around his neck and squeeze until his head popped off. I again handed off the questioning to my interview partner and excused myself. I paced back and forth out of sight of my partner and the man.

I told myself, *Breathe. Settle. Focus.*

Again, *Breathe. Settle. Focus.*

Again, *Breathe. Settle. Focus.*

Once more, *Breathe . . . Settle . . . Focus.*

After a few minutes I returned to the interview.

Calming myself down like this allowed me to stay in the room and listen. It allowed me to gather additional evidence to build a great case for the prosecutor. It was a reset so I could continue.

If you are wondering, the man is still in jail as I write this, and he is not able to hurt any children. That's a win.

7

I told the Wolf, "Okay, so, I know you've talked to several different people. I don't know all the people that you've talked to since you were arrested, but I have a couple questions since some things are not clear to me. Is that okay?"

He said, "Yes."

By now I had taken Morgan's advice, and I explained to those I interviewed how the interview would go. I did the same for the Wolf.

"Some of this may seem redundant, but since I wasn't present earlier, if I ask you something, it's because I don't know the answer. I also may ask some questions that may be personal or you may feel embarrassed to talk about. I am not trying to embarrass you. I am just trying to learn more about what happened. If that happens, I apologize ahead of time. I will ask most of the questions. My partner will be quiet most of the time. If we are quiet, we are not judging you for any reason, we are just listening to what you are sharing with us."

I raised my hand up like I was hitching a ride and pointed my thumb at the Kid.

"He will be writing some things down. He does that because there may be something he wants to ask you later and he doesn't want to forget. If you see him cross something off, it's because I asked a question that he wanted to ask."

The Wolf said, "Yep."

"What happened last night?"

"Um, well, I was talking online and went over to that house and got arrested, I guess."

"You got arrested. And why were you there again?"

"Um, to hook up with the mom and daughter, I guess."

"Mom and a daughter?"

"Yeah."

"How old was the daughter?"

"Um, she was just under twelve . . . eleven."

"So, eleven years old? Okay. Have you ever done anything like that before, hooked up with an eleven-year-old?"

"No, not an eleven-year-old."

I asked, "Not an eleven-year-old? What about any minors? Have you ever hooked up with any minors before?"

"Yes."

His answer surprised me. I wasn't expecting him to admit that.

"Yes. Okay, just so you know, by asking these questions, I'm not judging you in any way. I'm just trying to get an understanding of what happened. I have been doing this for about five years and I've heard pretty much everything you can think of or imagine."

I told him this again for a few reasons. First, so I remembered to settle. It was a way for me to keep my emotions in the box. Second, I would repeat this just in case my face deceived me and showed I was upset.

8

I wondered if he could sense my discomfort. It has happened to me a few times. Sometimes when I chatted in an undercover capacity I imagined where the conversation was going to take me. One time this happened and one of my detectives saw a change in my behavior.

They suggested we take a break and go for a walk. On our walk we talked about where I thought the conversation was going. She saw the moment I realized I was going to a dark place; she said I didn't look right. I'm glad she noticed because I didn't want to go where I thought this man wanted to go.

I spent about ten minutes talking with the detective and preparing my box. I was lucky to have her. She helped me get through that moment, and once I started to chat with the suspect, it wasn't as bad as I thought it was going to be.

9

When I went to those dark places, I became someone else—like acting without the cameras. We called the roles we played undercover personas. I transformed into a different person to protect children. In the following chapters you will get a peek into one of my undercover personas. As you read the rest of this book, remember, the words I typed and said do not represent who I am. I never wanted to go to those places. I don't think anybody that does this job ever wants to go there, but unfortunately it's a necessity.

When we conducted our undercover operations, we always had a safety briefing. During the briefing we went over the expectations and discussed the roles of each person participating in the operation. I made it a point to tell all involved that the text conversations between our undercovers and the suspects are difficult to read and are disgusting. I reminded them the undercover chatters were playing a role, and what they were typing was not who they really were. If the officers were at the briefing and not already chatting with a suspect, I would make eye contact with them while saying those words. Our eyes would meet, and they would nod to me with a small smile. I would nod back. It was important for everyone to realize they were playing a role.

When you work these crimes in an undercover capacity, you mimic the filth you are trying to clean up. Like I said, you go into dark places. I did my best to keep those dark places from holding on to my people.

10

The Wolf asked, "So, would it be smart for me to get a lawyer right now, or . . . ?"

Fuck yes, it would *be smart for you to get a lawyer right now, more like the moment you were read your rights yesterday.* But I said, "If you want a lawyer, yeah, you can get one. That's totally up to you."

"Okay."

"I can't advise you on that. That's not my role. That's totally up to you. If you don't want to talk to me anymore, that's fine. Is that it? Do you want to stop talking with me?"

He said, "I'm okay for now."

"You're okay? Now if you change your mind, you tell me, okay?"

"I will."

I asked, "So, what would you say would be the youngest?"

"Ten."

Box.

"Ten? And how old were you when that happened?"

"Thirty."

I thought, *You are thirty right now.* I continued, "Thirty? Was that the only time and was it one person?"

"It was two."

"Two people? And how old was the other one?"

"Twelve."

"Twelve? Now, are they related?"

"Yes."

"And are they related to you?"

"Yes."

"How are they related to you?"

"Stepdaughters."

"Stepdaughters? Okay. And what are their names?"

He told me the names of his stepdaughters. They were the same little girls from the search warrant scene.

Breathe. Settle. Focus.

I asked, "Twelve . . . so, when did that first start?"

He was so calm and matter-of-fact in his answers.

"A couple weeks ago, I guess."

"Couple weeks ago? And so, where was that?"

"Um, here in Lay—well in Lacey, Washington."

He corrected himself. The jail wasn't in Lacey, and I don't think he knew where he was except for in trouble.

I said, "In Lacey. Where did that take place at?"

"At my house."

"At your house? And where do you live? I don't know where you live."

The Wolf provided me with his address.

The timeline. I needed to start the timeline.

I said, "Lacey, Washington. Okay. Where were you born?"

The Wolf told me where he was from. He said he never met his father, but he had a good relationship with his mom.

"Did you have a similar relationship with your family like you had with the girls?"

He said, "No, I've never been abused."

I never said abused. That was all him. He acknowledged he had abused these little girls.

I said, "I don't like to call it abuse because people experience love in different ways. Some of those ways are not always morally accepted in every society. When you were growing up, did you have any relationships like that?"

He said, "No."

"No, nothing like that? What do you think brought you to where you had a relationship with the girls then?"

His dark little eyes met mine.

"I don't know."

He was lying.

"How did that start? What happened?"

"I don't know, just sort of happened, I guess."

Things like this don't just happen, you sick fuck. Okay, calm down. Breathe. Settle. Focus. "And again, I haven't talked to you up until this point, so when you said 'just sort of happened,' what is it that happened?"

"I guess . . ." The Wolf looked down and mumbled something. I couldn't hear him. He didn't want me to hear him.

"What's that?"

"We fooled around, I guess."

"You fooled around? So, was it both at the same time?"

He looked back up at me and then at the Kid. His voice was almost a whisper now. "No."

"No? So who was first?"

"Twelve."

"When you say fooled around, was it full penetration?"

"No."

"No? What was it?"

"A little bit of fingering, I guess."

Breathe. Settle. Focus. I continued, "Is that something that she wanted to do?"

"No."

"How did she respond to it?"

His eyes scanned back and forth between the Kid and me. He shook his head to the side to flip his hair out of his face.

"Kind of submissive, I guess."

I took a breath and let it out as I said, "Okay."

I continued, "Now, we're all people here, and people respond in different ways to being touched. I mean, that's just natural. That's how we're built. So usually when you touch somebody a certain way, they can get aroused. Is that something that happened? Did she get aroused when you touched her?"

"No."

"No? How did she respond?"

"Just sort of submissive, I guess. Just waited until it was over."

The Wolf continued to describe how he stole the innocence from his stepdaughters four to five times a month. How they lay motionless while he did what he wanted.

11

I was surprised this conversation was going so well.

"Were you afraid that maybe they would tell somebody?"

"Yes."

"What type of conversation did you have about that?"

He looked down at the table and said, "Nothing really."

I dug further. "So you never said anything?"

He looked back at me, flipping his hair out of his face again. "I told them to keep quiet, I guess, and try not to tell anybody."

"What'd they say?"

"Okay."

"Okay?"

"I never physically did anything or threatened ever, though."

There it was. Admission through denial. I didn't ask him if he ever hurt or threatened the girls to keep them quiet. The words flowed quickly out of his mouth as if telling us would make it okay.

Thanks for telling me that, that makes it all okay. How kind of you. I hoped he hadn't done anything to keep the girls quiet, but I didn't believe that at all.

We finished our interview, and the Wolf was taken back to his cell. The Kid and I went back to work.

I wish I could tell you the Wolf was the only person we arrested during this operation. He was not. The Wolf was only one of twenty-one persons seeking sex with children thirteen years and younger that we arrested that week.

12

Nearly a week later, the girls agreed to be interviewed at the local Child Advocacy Center (CAC). When our task force believed a child had been abused or was experiencing abuse, the child was brought to a CAC by a caregiver or other "safe" adult. The CAC is a safe, child-focused environment. At the CAC, the child tells their story once to a trained interviewer who knows the right questions to ask so they do not retraumatize the child.

Most CACs have a team that includes medical, law enforcement, mental health, prosecution, victim advocacy, and other professionals that can help the child based on the interview.

Without a CAC, the child may end up telling the worst story of their life over and over again, to doctors, cops, lawyers, therapists, investigators, judges, and others. CACs minimize the child having to repeat that nightmare multiple times.

The girls were scheduled to be interviewed by a detective named Holly. Normally the forensic interviewers were civilians, but they were not available. Holly was their backup. This worried me—not because she wasn't qualified to conduct the interview but because Holly and I did not get along.

Holly worked for a different agency. When my task force worked with her, I thought she was stubborn and not a team player. She was not willing to accept help from her peers and tried to work cases on her own. In my opinion this wasn't good for anyone and ultimately worked against our mission.

When I first met Holly, she was a new detective, and my task force was asked to assist her with a case. I don't know if she was trying to prove a point by not asking for help, but she was fucking up the case, and her ego was hindering our investigation.

This meant a sixteen-year-old trafficking victim might not get the justice she deserved. After my attempts to work with her failed, I set a meeting with her command staff to discuss my concerns. They agreed with me and transferred the case to my task force. Holly was directed to assist us. She didn't like the outcome, and when we crossed paths after that, she simply ignored me.

13

I arrived at the CAC. Holly was sitting in a small room decorated like a kindergarten classroom. The room was designed to help children feel comfortable. It had stuffed animals, toys, crayons, and kid-sized furniture. There was a camera on one of the walls, and its feed was sent to a viewing room where I could watch the interview. If I thought something might have been missed, I could pass along any questions I wanted Holly to ask. She would then ask the questions only if she felt it was appropriate to do so.

I was standing in the hallway when Holly noticed me. I nodded to her, saying, "Holly."

She looked away from me and studied what looked like a case report. "Carlos."

Yup, she hates me.

I continued to the viewing room. The camera feed was displayed on a small monitor for me to view. I saw the twelve-year-old girl walk in and sit down across from Holly. My heart sunk.

God, she was so tiny and paper thin, weighing maybe fifty to sixty pounds. As she sat down, she pushed her glasses back up onto her nose. Her voice was soft. Her arms were folded tightly around her little torso and she crossed her legs at the ankles.

The little girl scanned the room. She looked at Holly, but only for a few seconds at a time. Holly began to talk with her. As they spoke, the little girl didn't scan the room as much and began to focus on Holly. As the little girl relaxed, I began to relax.

That lasted for only a few minutes. Not because of Holly, but because of what I was about to hear.

14

Holly asked the little girl, "Why do you think you are here?"

The little girl looked at her and then down at her feet. "'Cause my dad did something really stupid." The little girl said she didn't know what he did, but she knew it wasn't good.

Holly asked, "Do you have any rules in your house?"

"Yeah, we have chores, and we have a rule to tell the truth."

"Can you tell me about that rule, to tell the truth?"

"Me and my sisters used to not tell the truth sometimes and so we have that rule, so we tell the truth now."

The little girl described her likes and dislikes about her family. She wished her mom didn't work as much and that her stepdad would work more. She didn't like when she fought with her sister, but it wasn't ever really bad.

The little girl liked Holly; she was opening up to her.

Holly asked, "Is there anything about your house that makes you feel unsafe or uncomfortable?"

"My dad has swords."

She looked back down at her feet. The room went quiet.

No questions, no answers. Only silence.

The little girl fidgeted with her hands like she had something in them, but there was nothing there. She peeked at Holly like she wasn't sure if she was still in the room, then her gaze went back down at her hands. She said quietly, "Nobody in my house does anything to my body that makes me feel unsafe or uncomfortable."

Holly paused and then said, "Do you have any idea what your dad did or why you aren't with your mom?"

"I don't know."

The little girl was rolling the bottom of her shirt with her tiny fingers. Her voice trembled. "When the police came to my house around two in the morning, I felt scared for my dad." A few tears made their way down her face. "I'm just missing my mom."

"Your mom is safe, sweetie. Someone told us there was stuff in your house that was unsafe or uncomfortable for you and your sister."

The tears were now flowing down her face and onto her shirt. "I just miss her."

"Your mom is safe. Sometimes people make mistakes. The important thing now is to talk about the truth." Holly paused and then said, "I want you to know I know what happened in your house that makes you unsafe."

The little girl nodded.

Holly said, "What do you think I am talking about when I said you are not safe?"

She said, "How my dad sexually harasses me and my little sister."

"Can you tell me about it?"

"Yeah. He only married my mom just for me and my little sister, that's what he told us. He said if we told anyone he would hurt us."

The twelve-year-old detailed how her dad started "sexually harassing" her two years prior when they lived in another state. She said she couldn't remember all the details since she had suffered a concussion from the first time.

She talked about what she remembered. "Ummm . . . he would, like . . . you know when those girls get, like, taken and raped? Kind of like that."

Holly was so focused.

"What do you mean by taken and raped? Was it violent?"

"Kind of. If we didn't do what he liked, he would choke us. He choked me twice. I didn't want to do what he was wanting me to do, so he choked me."

"What did he want you to do?"

"Take off my clothes."

She described how the Wolf would "choke slam" them by grabbing their throats and slamming them into the ground. She said the last time he raped her was a month ago.

She continued to describe sinister things that should never happen to anybody, let alone this little girl and her sister.

I imagined myself back at the jail grabbing the Wolf by his little neck and seeing how he liked being "choke slammed."

She continued to cry while she told what her dad did to her.

15

The interview was over. Holly stepped out of the room and poked her head into the room the prosecutor and I were in.

Our eyes met. We forced small smiles onto our faces. "Holly, thank you."

"Yup."

"No, I mean it. Thank you."

She nodded.

Breathe. Settle. Focus.

This hit me differently. I started to shut down. Time slowed. I knew I needed to get up, but I was frozen. I wondered if the others in the room noticed I wasn't moving. The prosecutor was talking to me. I could hear her voice, but I couldn't understand what she was saying. I thought, *What are you saying?*

In that moment nothing made sense. I needed to regulate, to reset. *Breathe. Settle. Focus.*

I searched for a box, but I did not have the space for this. I was able to get up from my chair. I said, "Um, I have to get something from my car."

I was talking too fast; I felt they were going to notice. I told myself, *Slow your words.*

The prosecutor stepped into the hallway with me.

I said, "I'll be right back, it won't take me that long." I was in a panic to leave. My voice felt funny; I thought, *She knows. They know.*

The prosecutor did know. It must have been all over my face. She said, "Carlos, before you go, I need to talk to you." She put her hand on my shoulder and directed me into her office. I remember her closing her door. Tears were running down my face now.

"I'm . . . um, I'm . . . I'm sorry. I just need a quick minute."

She raised her arms to me, offering a hug. I didn't hug prosecutors, but I took it. I began to sob. "I just can't. I . . . I can't. I just need a second, I'm usually good about this."

I quickly separated from her. I needed to get out.

"Carlos, it's okay. You did your part. It's my turn now."

I stood still.

She said, "I will fight to make sure he gets what he deserves. Know that."

I said, "She is sooo small."

I don't think I made sense. The taste of salt told me to wipe the tears from my face.

Breathe. Settle. Focus.

I found a new, bigger box.

16

I lost control. My emotions got the best of me. I saw that as a failure on my part. I was embarrassed.

How odd it must have been for the prosecutor. Not because I lost control. How strange to watch a man go from sobbing uncontrollably to taking a breath and just stopping. I just turned it off.

I said, "Thanks. I'll call you later."

The prosecutor made good on her word. She did what she set out to do. The Wolf pled guilty to all counts and was sentenced to eighteen years to life.

FOURTEEN

THE PRICE OF YES

1

Saying no to helping others was difficult for me. This translated to being away from home a lot. Julie handled most everything for the kids in my absence. When someone called, I answered. Sometimes I would watch my phone play tag with loose change while it vibrated on my nightstand. *It can wait until tomorrow.* Then my inside voice would say, *Can it?*

The voice has always been there, telling me what to do, warning what will happen if I don't help. When I worked nights as a trooper, I usually made it home late. If I saw a car struggling to stay within its lane, I would stop it. After all, it could be a drunk. The senior troopers told me, "Put the blinders on, kid," which meant ignore the car and get home. I never did that. *If you don't check, they are gonna kill someone. They are gonna kill someone's David.* I listened to the voice and always made the stop, just like I always answered the phone. Instead of stopping drunk drivers, I was helping protect a kid or work a case to put the evil away.

2

Julie was great about keeping me in the loop with what was going on with the kids, mostly through text messages, or emails if it was something from the school I needed to read. My response was usually: "That works," "You're the best!," or "I like that answer, I'll be home late, gotta go."

If I didn't agree with something or something went wrong, I would blame her for not knowing or "allowing" it to happen. I don't have an explanation for why I did that; I just know I did and know now it wasn't fair to her.

Julie didn't message or call me while I was working unless it had a timeline attached to it or it was an emergency. That was great for my casework but a negative for our relationship. It got worse when the Net Nanny operations started in August of 2015. We began to lose each other. My focus shifted more and more to the operations and away from Julie and the kids. Julie's focus never shifted. It was always on us. It didn't matter what was happening in our lives. She sacrificed a lot for us.

3

To make matters worse, my plan to shield Julie and the kids from the Ugly was flawed. The safety plan for them may have distanced them from the Ugly, but it also took me away from them.

"Hey guys! I'm home. I'm gonna work on some stuff really quick, I'll be downstairs for a bit."

It was never quick. After we had talked for a few minutes, I would scurry down the stairs into our basement and sit at my desk. Sometimes I had work; other times I would simply sit in silence.

I lost my ability to relax. I was never still and was constantly moving. I was like a little boy doing the pee dance. When we went to family/friend functions, I was restless. I would mingle for a bit while scanning the room for the best place to escape. I would move to a chair in a corner or maybe sneak into another room—places where I didn't have to talk with anyone. When I did interact with people, they usually asked me about the parts of my job that I didn't want to or couldn't talk about. What I really wanted was to go home and lose myself by climbing into my king-sized bed, by watching a movie, or via sleep. When I did finally lie down, the voice and I worked out what the next day looked like. Eventually I would fall asleep.

4

We did make time for vacations, but the more time I spent in the Ugly, the less I wanted to leave for vacations.

Julie would text me:

> June 29–July 8? Anytime in that time frame?

> I can do the 27th through the 6th

> and only burn 3 days of leave.

I planned everything around work. When we went on vacation, it took a while to settle in. The first few days consisted of me stressing about all the things I wasn't doing instead of focusing on where I was. I was with my family physically but not mentally. Present without being present. By day three I could relax. Day four or five is when I started to think about all the things I needed to do when I got back.

Julie didn't give up on me, though. She reminded me to be there with them. She was good at bringing me back, but that became harder with time. It wasn't like this on every vacation, though. When we went to Disney World, it was different.

Disney World reminded me of when my parents were happy together, when we lived in Oklahoma, before my parents divorced. My dad would pack us into his little brown 1981 Honda Civic hatchback and drive us to a timeshare in Kissimmee, Florida. We would go to Disney World for a week almost every year. I have no bad memories from there. I don't know how my parents pulled it off because we didn't have a lot of money, but they figured it out. We were happy there, and it was no different for Julie, the kids, and me years later. So many smiles.

Oddly enough, my favorite family vacation didn't involve Disney.

5

I ran into my house looking for Julie. I heard Julie's mouse-clicking coming from the loft area at the top of the stairs. I yelled up to her, "Honey, let's drive to the Grand Canyon."

The clicking stopped. Julie looked down at me with a confused smile. "Okay!"

It was early March 2016, and I had wrapped up our third Net Nanny operation. I was having a difficult time with some of the subject matter from two separate suspects from this operation. The first was a man I mentioned earlier—the one I struggled to remain composed with and had to take a break from during the interview. The second case involved a man offering up his own daughters for sex and wanting to have sex with preteen girls. The Ugly wasn't going quietly into its box. I needed to settle—better yet, escape.

"Yeah?"

"Yes!"

"All right, let's get out of here."

I love road trips, and I had never been to the Grand Canyon. For the next few hours I immersed myself in planning our trip. *This is going to be the trip of all trips, not just the Grand Canyon, but a history lesson on how Dad grew up.* My plan was to drive from Puyallup, Washington, to Palm Springs, California, where we would stay a day to soak up some sun and swim in a pool. I thought a day or two would be enough at the Grand Canyon. From there we would drive to Colorado Springs, Colorado, where I used to live. I wanted to show the kids my old house and visit Garden of the Gods. My mom took my sister and me there when we were little. The next phase was to drive through Wyoming, Montana, Idaho, and then back to Washington, all the while stopping at quirky little spots and eating whatever we wanted at greasy spoons. I was crazy to think we could do it all, plus we didn't have the budget to do half of it.

6

"It's all right, Dad." My daughter could tell I was upset. Two hours into our trip we had car trouble and had to turn back. I was pissed because in my mind we were losing four to five hours and our other car wasn't as fuel efficient. That cut into our budget and meant less money to do all the sites.

"We're gonna have fun." I looked in the rearview mirror and found Liv's eyes smiling at me. In that moment that's all I needed.

"Yes, we are, Boo Boo."

Most of us made a playlist to listen to, except for Liv. When it was her turn, she plugged the AUX cord into her phone. Blue Swede's "Hooked on a Feeling" filled the car. "Crank it, Dad." Her playlist was the *Guardians of the Galaxy* volume 1 soundtrack. We listened and sang along to that soundtrack the entire trip.

We made it to Palm Springs, played in the pool, saw the canyon, and ate as much as we wanted. After the Grand Canyon we made our way back to the Pacific Northwest. On the way back, instead of staying on Interstate 5, we veered off toward the Pacific Coast. We stopped at the Jelly Belly factory and learned how jelly beans were made. Then we continued toward the coast and drove through the Redwoods on US 101. We were able to catch the sunset on the beach just north of Trinidad, California. Yes, this work did a number on me, but that trip—that trip was perfection.

FIFTEEN

PRINCESS

> **CONTENT WARNING**
>
> As noted on the copyright page, while adults should be free to review any of this material and may find it to be informative, reader discretion is advised. This chapter contains content about criminal sexual activities involving children that may be offensive to some adults and is inappropriate for minors.

1

On February 20, 2019, we had just wrapped up our fifteenth Net Nanny operation. It was three years and ten operations later since we had arrested the Wolf. I thought by this time we wouldn't be able to arrest anybody else in this fashion, but I was wrong.

When we first started these operations, we worked what seemed like around the clock. I survived on two to three hours of sleep and managed to stay upright with the help of Bang peach mango energy drinks and Starbucks trenta black iced teas. Running an operation on minimal sleep four to five days in a row is not healthy.

With each operation we would learn how to do things better.

We identified two things that had had the most negative effect on our operations: lack of resources and fatigue. These two things are connected. When we had more resources, our fatigue was minimized.

Most think of resources as inanimate objects such as equipment, software, training, or funding. Those are all important, but the most important resource I had was my people. If I took care of them, then everything else fell into place. As we conducted more operations around the state, more people wanted us to run operations in their communities. This created an opportunity to build a team with friends who had the skill sets to enhance future operations, which then allowed us to schedule more staff, reduce our overtime, and minimize the fatigue.

We would stop around a certain time most nights so we were fresh enough to start the next day. If we identified a target that didn't follow our schedule, we put together a smaller team to focus on that target while the rest of the team rested for the next day. Eventually we had enough help so we could arrest multiple targets at different locations at the same time.

We continued to do these operations because people continued to show up wanting to rape children thirteen years old and younger. We were averaging seven arrests a night, and this Net Nanny was no different. We had arrested twenty-two people seeking to rape children ages six through thirteen.

At this point we had arrested 246 men and women and had removed more than thirty children from harm across Washington state through our Net Nanny operations. With enough funding and mental fortitude, we had enough cases to work these operations around the clock.

2

My phone rang.

"Sergeant Rodriguez."

"Los, I know you are on an op, but hear me out."

It was Madson. He was a part of the FBI SSCETF, and we had worked on some cases together. When I helped him, it was mostly interviewing potential trafficked persons or as close cover for his human trafficking operations.

Madson worked for a local city PD and worked mostly sex trafficking cases. He reminded me of Woody from *Toy Story* but without the cowboy outfit. He isn't goofy like that, just lanky and has those big Woody eyes.

I said, "Man, I'm slammed. I'm prepping case files for the prosecutor." The last thing I wanted at that moment was a new case.

"Los . . ."

"Seriously, man, I have a lot of shit to do."

"Just hear me out on this one, that's all I ask."

"I have twenty-two cases to put together, man."

This is the part where my mind goes down the rabbit hole. My mind shows me a small child being tormented over and over. It tells me it's happening because I chose not to help. My mind tells me, *If you do nothing, it's your fault.* This is followed by a quick body shake to get the idea out of my head. The images fade, but the thought of it lingers.

This was no different. I said, "Okay, I'm listening."

Madson said, "I have a CI that went on a date with this chick. We were looking at her for trafficking a minor, but then she said some fucked-up shit. Thing is, she is looking for a connect that has kids. She wants to fuck kids while they are drugged. That's your thing, man, not mine. You're the expert on that shit, and I need your help. I know you are slammed—"

I interrupted him. "Hey, I'm in." I thought, *Really? My thing? It's not my thing.* But I knew what he meant. "I'll get you a number to give the CI."

"Thanks, Los."

"No problem, man. Thanks for calling me. Call me tomorrow, I have to finish this shit."

The next day Madson filled me in on the target. Princess was twenty-two years old, and Madson suspected she was trafficking a sixteen-year-old runaway. His CI said Princess had pics and videos of snakes and mice being hurt. This told me she most likely was a sadist. It also told me she might not be sexually attracted to kids but more into gaining power and control over them. I imagined she got off on their pain. She wanted them drugged. I didn't know if that was because it would be easier for her to manage them or if it was just a part of a sick fantasy.

Get your head straight.

I learned over the years the necessity of considering all things possible but to keep an open mind. If I began a conversation with someone and had a predetermined opinion of who they were, I would most definitely miss something.

I was getting ahead of myself. I needed to focus on who I was about to become in a few hours.

3

Before we go to another dark place, I want to talk about personas again, but these are not the undercover personas we talked about earlier. These personas are ones that we all use every day of our lives.

A persona can be the image or personality that a person presents in public or in a special setting as opposed to their true self. It can also refer to a fictional character or role that a person adopts.

Everyone has different personas. Let's use me as an example. I have multiple personas. When I am at work, I interact with the public based on what is appropriate in that setting. Although we don't have a dress code, I still dress and communicate with those around me a certain way. I do this so I am perceived in a good light.

When I'm around those that I am close with, like friends and family, I am more relaxed, and my guard isn't up as much as it is when I am in public.

Finally, when I am alone, I do things that I wouldn't necessarily do around others, things that I may be embarrassed to do in front of others. It could be scratching an itch in a private area, passing gas, or singing to my cat.

For some, it could be an embarrassing habit or a disorder like depression or negative thoughts.

When working crimes against children, I learned people that are sexually attracted to kids create personas to avoid detection. Think about it. How many times have you seen a TV news interview and heard, "He was such a nice man. I can't believe it."

Child predators create an image of themselves to blend in and appear "normal." They do this to create an opportunity to get what they want. For my law enforcement family that are doing this work, the training I mentioned earlier in this book by Dr. Joe Sullivan will help you identify different personas in your interviews as well as when you are communicating with suspects online. Again, if you have not taken the course, I highly recommend you take the training.[3]

---

3   Forensic Solutions (website), accessed August 2, 2025, www.forensicsolutions.com.

4

When working child abuse cases, we used cold devices. Cold devices are computers, iPads, or phones we used strictly for undercover purposes. This was to minimize a suspect's ability to detect we were law enforcement. I don't know why we called them cold devices. I like to think it's like the game most of us played as a kid when we are searching for something. You are hot when you are close to discovering it and cold when you are far away. It's funny how I never really thought about it until right now.

The phone number provided to the CI was created for this case by a software program designed for undercover law enforcement investigations. I used this software to text with Princess.

I have included some of the text conversations between Princess and my UC persona. Again, this can get dark, so please prepare yourself mentally.

My persona's texts are on the right. Princess's texts are on the left.

> Hey, is this Princess?

> This is Donnies friend Ryan.

Donnie was the CI's name.

Hi Ryan! Yes this is ☺

How may I service you?

> He said you had a trade for my littles.

Yes. Would you be able to send pic?

I didn't want to send her a pic, not yet. I wanted to wait for a bit and see what she would offer up.

I will do anything you want

Falling asleep. Feel free to text, I'll answer in the morning.

I typed,

I have two.

I attached a photo of what looked like a twelve-year-old little girl taking a selfie. The photo was of a young-looking state trooper. She used a filter that added little teddy bear ears and some black-rimmed glasses to her head and face.

I thought, *That should do the trick* and sent the message.

Less than a minute later Princess replied,

Ooh she's cute!
Are they virgins?

Now that I had piqued her interest, I needed to find out about the runaway.

Tell me about yours

Did Donnie say I have kids?
I don't have kids.

I can give you my pussy and time.
Have you join and help me 😈

He said you had a young one.
Idk. I like young.

Tell me what you want to
make sure I have what you want.

We continued to chat. I made it clear I wasn't interested in having sex with her or any other adult. Princess needed to understand the person she was texting with was only interested in having sex with children.

I need proof that I'm not going to get in trouble.
Can you send a nude of a little?

If you have one, then I'll tell you exactly
what I want to do to your cute daughter.

This was a common request. It was also a request I never fulfilled. First off, I wasn't going to send CSAM to her. Also, that's how hundreds of people that trade CSAM get caught.

Donnie already told me.
I know what you want dirty girl.

He said you had a girl for me.

Sending a nude of my littles
is how you get in trouble silly.

If you have what I want,
I have what you need.

It's not safe to do what you said.

HMU 2morro and maybe it will work out.

I stopped texting with her close to midnight. My body needed rest. I also needed to spend about thirty minutes to an hour doing something totally different before I went to bed. I didn't want our conversations in my head as I fell asleep. If Princess was serious, she would text me back. She would text me back because I had what she wanted.

5

The next morning Princess began texting around 6:30 a.m. She must have been dreaming about it all night.

I might have a girl for you. But she's 16.

Yes I am a dirty girl,

I want to give your daughter
medicine to help her sleep.
Then I'm going to give her lots of kisses

I'll be super gentle

♡ I want to kiss her tits and make
my way down to my favorite parts.

I won't destroy her, I'll just use my mouth and fingers.

As I read her texts I thought, *Sick fuck.*

That's better. Can you send a pic?

Yes

Of myself or the girl?

Princess sending a pic of herself would be a bonus; I meant a pic of the girl so I could see if it was Madson's runaway or not.

Both if you want, but for sure the girl.

Again, I needed to make it clear I wasn't interested in Princess sexually, and having sex with me was not an option. This was about the kids.

How thin is she. I like little.

Princess sent a photo of the runaway as well as one of herself along with the text,

Nope I'm a perv

I thought, *Yes you are.*
Princess began to ask about my younger daughter, "Tiny."

What can I do with tiny?
I like new though . . .

"New" meant she wanted virgins.

My oldest just turned 13, Tiny is 11.

Tiny is newer.

Are you clean?

I have sleepytime medicine, but
you will need to be more careful/slow
with tiny since she is new.

I like tiny. I will go slow and gentle.

It does not turn me on to cause damage.

I thought, *Liar*. She wanted them drugged so they couldn't tell
on her.

I just want tiny. The other one
is too old for my liking.

What will you give me if you
don't have the girl to trade for?

TBH this sounds sketch.

I wanted Princess to believe I was worried about losing my girls and I was not sold on meeting with her yet.

Fat Donnie told me you had a girl and now you don't. Idk.

If you don't have the girl I want $$ for the medicine and time with tiny.

Donnie doesn't think before he talks.

How much money are you looking for? 150?

Seriously

She is 11, its at least double that to start.

I have more at risk than you.

Usually I only deal with people I know and I'm already not doing what I normally do but only cuz I know donnie.

Seems fair.

I'm at work rn,

let me get back to you later today.

Kk, I work too so if I dont txt back thats why.

Don't call. Txt only unless we agree on calling. Safer for us both that way.

6

Princess and I continued to chat over the next few days. I wanted to know more about her.

Things like:

- Was she raised this way?

- Had she done this before with kids?

- Did someone do this to her?

Princess told me she came from a split family, and she didn't know her dad until she was about fourteen years old. When she reunited with her dad, they "participated in fun together" on a nightly basis. Her mother was extremely religious, which caused Princess "to rebel more and bring out what was already inside of me. All the desires." Princess admitted to "playing" with a younger cousin while she was sleeping.

I have a few rules.

OK

Be honest about what you want.

That way there are no surprises and I can tell you if it is safe for them.

I'd like to use a small glass dildo and ease it in slowly, I'd like to use fingers and mouth primarily.

That should be fine. Are you clean?

Yes I am clean. In a LTR.
They are unaware of my desires.

LTR means: long-term relationship.

Good. stds bring questions.

I can't have that.

How long have u been searching?

I've been looking for a few years.

Our conversation continued. As the days went on, her desires became more detailed. She decided she wanted the older girl as well since she would be able to handle more.

Princess asked if she was giving a donation. A donation in the world of sex trafficking is the fee paid for the sex act. Yes. She would be giving a donation.

Princess started to ask questions about what I looked like.

May I have a picture of you?

Why

That's a good point, NVM

I mean you know it's not about sex with me right.

Again, I needed to make it clear I wasn't offering for her to have sex with an adult. There must be no doubt for a judge or jury about what this was: Princess paying to rape two drugged-up kids.

Yes. I was just curious about how the dad looked

Kk I'm a little eccentric.

I usually wear eyeliner.

Okay, did I need to say that? Absolutely not. Thing is this is some dark shit and sometimes I needed to find a way to laugh. I called Madson. "Hey, man. I'm chatting with Princess. I need a pic of you."

Madson was hyped. "Okay, man, no problem!"

"Yeah, make sure you put on some eyeliner."

"Fuck off, man."

"I'm serious, man. Eyeliner. Thick enough so it shows up in the pic."

"What the fuck, man? Are you serious?"

I said, "For the children."

Madson said, "Okay."

Madson borrowed some of his wife's eyeliner and sent the pics. He decided to slide into a white tank top and skinny jeans. Picture a young Freddy Mercury. It was perfect.

7

Six days after Princess and I began chatting, she decided it was time to meet the girls.

What day and time works best for you and what am I paying?

Today through Thursday works

Price? $100 per girl?

Do you still want them sleeping?

How much do you have?

I have $200 cash on me.

I want them sleeping.
Not awake. Too sketchy.

I can do that if I get to watch.

You can watch. I could come today.

Be there by 11. Need address.

I started making calls to put a team together while I was chatting with Princess. Within thirty minutes we had a mix of WSP, FBI, and Lakewood police detectives to help with surveillance, arrest, and digital forensics. It's funny how quickly people clear their schedules when I ask, "Wanna help arrest someone who wants to drug two kids and have sex with them?"

I continued to text with Princess as I planned her arrest.

11 or noon is good. Txt when you leave.

R u excited?

Very excited and scared this
is fake, but really want to do it.

I said to myself, *I bet you do.*

This 💯 real.

KK

I couldnt get the house, but I got
a place near the South Hill Mall.

I dont have it till noon though.

It was 8 a.m. I figured meeting at noon would give me enough time to brief the team and get them in place.

Does that work I need 2 know cuz
I have to give them medicine
to make sure they are asleep.

South Hill is a little far
You couldn't find Tacoma?

I didn't answer her question. I was banking on her showing because I had what she wanted. Eight seconds later she responded.

I will drive to South Hill though if I need to

8

I briefed the team on the plan. We went over everyone's roles and answered any questions that any of us had.

We secured a suite at a popular hotel near State Route 512. We had plenty of time for the team to familiarize themselves with the area and work through any safety concerns. We knew once Princess left Bremerton, Washington, we had about an hour before she reached us. That's if she was actually in Bremerton.

To maintain operational integrity, I didn't give Princess the address of the hotel. I waited until we were in place and ready for her.

This hotel shares a parking lot with a restaurant I took my kids to and my favorite bakery. This was happening in my neighborhood. In my backyard, so to speak.

People asked me a lot if I was afraid of running into people I had arrested when I was off work. The answer is: Not as much as I used to be.

In the past if I ran into somebody when I was off, they knew I was alone and not working because I didn't have a uniform on. Working in plain clothes was different.

When a person or persons recognized me, their eyes scanned the area, searching for the rest of my team. I felt safer than when I was in uniform because I had more time to think and consider my response.

This dynamic changed when I was out with my family. As my children grew older, I went over safety precautions with them. We had a plan for our home as well as for when we were in public. We went over the plan about once a month. Sometimes we would just do scenarios while driving in the car.

My kids knew if I told them, "Hey, right now is a good time for you to stand over there," they needed to get a safe distance away from me and watch to see when to come back. If they saw something go down, they were supposed to run and get help. If it was more serious, I would address the threat as needed or I would just tell them to run and get help and we wouldn't use that code phrase. The first time I had to implement this I was with my son, Noah.

9

Noah was eight years old and was helping me with a large yard project. It was a doozy; I took a week's vacation to get it done. We removed brush from our front and backyard and then built a raised garden area using large retaining wall blocks. Noah helped me set the large twelve-inch pewter blocks. Each block weighed about twenty pounds, which was at least a third of his weight. Once we were finished with the raised area, we filled it with garden soil. After that we spread pea gravel all over the areas that we had cleared.

When we finally finished, we tossed our shovels and lay down on the lawn in the backyard. Diego, one of our three little chihuahuas, joined us. He had markings like a Jack Russell, but he was all chihuahua. All three of us lay on our backs and stared at the clouds. Well,

Noah and I did. Diego snorted and rubbed against us. That was his way of demanding a belly rub.

It felt good to just lie there.

Noah and I were wearing plain white T-shirts, blue jeans, and brown Romeos. We were caked in dirt from head to toe.

I looked over at Noah and said, "Bub, no way I got this done without you. Do you wanna get something from the store?"

Most kids would get amped, but not Noah. "Well, I do think we deserve some root beer, Dad."

He was right. We did. We didn't keep soda in the house—too much sugar and my kids would drink them all in a couple of days. Noah loved Henry Weinhard sodas. He was smart opening with the root beer since he knew that's the only soda I still liked.

"Can I go with you, Dad?"

"Of course, Bub. You have to pick out what you want. Let's go change first."

Noah ran to the back sliding glass door and kicked off his Romeos before running into the house. He was yelling for his mom to tell her he was going to the store before he even got through the sliding glass door. Watching him reminded me of my dad taking me to the store. Instead of soda, though, it was Hershey's chocolate bars with almonds.

We both cleaned up and put on some new clothes. Our T-shirts and jeans didn't match this time, but our shoes did—black-and-cream checkerboard Vans. No socks.

We jumped in the van, drove to the nearest Safeway, and walked directly to the aisle with the specialty sodas. Noah couldn't stand still. His legs twisted tightly around each other like the neck of a wire coat hanger. He kept bouncing up and down.

"Noah, do you have to pee?"

"Not yet, Dad."

He was muttering to himself, "Root beer, cream soda, root beer, cream . . ."

"Noah, how about I get a root beer, and you get . . ."

As I was talking to him, I noticed a man and woman bundled in puffy jackets walking toward us. They stuck out because it was hot outside. Streaks of ketchup and mustard were painted onto the lower part of their jackets and the thighs of their jeans. I figured they had just come from the Burger King that was in the same lot as the Safeway.

The man looked at me and then grabbed the woman's arm, stopping her about twenty feet away from us. He continued to look at me while he talked to the woman. I suspected he told her not to look at me since she immediately turned her head to see me. Her eyes met mine and she quickly turned back toward the man.

I thought, *Fuck. That's Sean.*

10

I had arrested Sean for selling and distributing large amounts of OxyContin and cannabis about three years earlier. After his arrest, Sean agreed to work for me as a confidential informant. He did not fulfill his contract. That meant he went to prison.

I didn't know the woman. Sean continued to talk to her as she picked at some of the dried mustard on her jeans.

You two should be shopping for laundry detergent, not soda.

Breathe. Settle. Focus.

Noah didn't notice anything. He was still deciding on which soda to get. I bent down next to him and whispered, "Noah."

He wasn't listening to me. I placed my hands on his arms to hold him still and said, "Noah. Hey, Bub, look at me."

He pretended to be frozen. His eyes were wide and his mouth open, but still smiling. He was looking at me but not looking at me.

I whispered, "Noah, right now is a good time for you to go stand over there."

Noah threw his shoulders back and gave me his best Macaulay Culkin *Home Alone* face. "Right now?"

"Yes. Right now. Go."

I didn't think the little guy would be so excited. I could see the classic waffle soles of his Vans as he raced to the end of the aisle. He was sprinting like he just hit a line drive and had to make it to first base. He stopped quickly at the end of the aisle and set up to steal second. He looked back at me and waited for my signal.

The couple was now standing five feet away from me.

"Hey, Sean."

"Hey, Los, thought that was you."

His lips were chapped, like he was using dried skin as lip liner. I found myself licking my own lips as if chapped lips were contagious. His face looked like a skull wrapped in blotchy skin. Sean didn't have many teeth left, and those that were still in his mouth were going to retire soon. He smelled like a towel does when it's left in the washing machine too long. I breathed through my mouth instead of my nose to keep from smelling him.

"We aren't gonna have a problem, are we, Sean?"

He was focused on Noah. "Is that your kid?"

No shit it's my kid. Noah looked just like me but with lighter hair.

"Sean." He turned his attention away from Noah. "Are YOU going to have a problem today?"

"No. I just wanted to say thanks for giving me a chance."

I wasn't expecting him to say that.

Sean continued, "I messed up and got locked up. You gave me a chance, but I fucked that up. When I got out, I called your cell, but it wasn't you. The guy who answered told me you went to a different job. I don't know if you knew or not, I mean, that I went in."

It's an uncomfortable feeling when someone you put in prison tells you they talk about you. I don't think I will ever get used to that.

"Well, we tried, right?"

"Yeah, I'm good now. This is my girlfriend." He said her name. "She keeps me out of trouble."

Sean's definition of trouble was different than mine since Sean looked like he was currently in trouble.

"That's good."

Sean and the woman turned around. I glanced over at Noah and showed him the palm of my hand, directing him to stay put. He gave me a confident nod and waited for my next signal.

Sean and his girlfriend left the store. I signaled Noah to run back to me, to his home base. When he got to me, he wrapped his arms around my legs and almost knocked me over. His sweaty face stuck to my jeans.

"You did good, Bub! I say root beer *and* cream soda. What do you think?"

"Was that a bad guy, Dad?"

"No, just a guy that made a bad decision."

"Did you see me, Dad? I was ready!"

"Yes you were, Bub."

We were lucky; this could have gone much differently. I am fortunate nothing ever happened to any of my family. This scenario was not ideal, but we had a plan prepared, and luckily it worked out. There were a few more times like this one when my kids were older, but they knew what to do. We had drilled this many times, and when the time came, they responded appropriately. The other times the suspects didn't even notice us. That was because I was lucky enough to see them before they saw me and we were able to avoid them.

As you can imagine, this line of work could be traumatic and stressful for my family members. Especially when there are people that wanted to do me harm. We were lucky it worked out for us. We also minimized some of the stress by talking through scenarios and planning for the worst.

I didn't plan for something bad to happen. I just knew if I didn't plan, something bad would happen.

11

Surveillance was in the lot. Everyone else was in place to detain Princess. The hotel suite was recently renovated. It consisted of a small kitchenette, a sleeper sofa, a separate bedroom, and a small bathroom. The bedroom and bathroom areas were hidden behind two French doors.

Madson paced in front of the sofa. He was already in character as Daddy Eyeliner. Special Agent Ted Bennett and I were in the bedroom area of the suite along with the arrest team. Princess stopped to pick up cash, lube, and some Cool Ranch Doritos. I checked one more time to make sure we were all in place. This was it. I sent her our location and the room number.

At this point in my career, I had done this hundreds of times. Even so, my stomach ached, my heart raced, and I wondered, *Will she show? If she doesn't, who will she find to feed her appetite?"*

At about 12:20 p.m., surveillance units started to buzz over the radio.

Unit 1: I have a green Kia Soul pulling into the lot.

Unit 2: Copy that.

Unit 3: Confirmation on the target; looks like she is making a few passes.

That meant she was looking for surveillance units. We called that countersurveillance.

Unit 3: Target parked. Exiting. Headed toward the entrance.

Units 1 and 2: Copy.

Unit 3: Black leggings, black top with brown flower pattern, brown boots. Target has a black backpack and a grocery bag.

Unit 1: Keep one on the Kia.

Unit 2: I'll stay with the car.

Unit 3: I lost the eye.

Unit 4: I have the eye; she is in the lobby headed to the elevator.

Unit 4: In elevator. I don't have the eye. Target should be headed to the room.

Unit 1: All units stay in position until we get confirmation from the arrest team.

All units: Copy.

My stomach no longer ached. This was happening.

Breathe. Settle. Focus.

I heard several knocks coming from the other room and then heard the front door open. I struggled to hear what Madson and Princess were saying. I held my breath thinking that would improve my chances of hearing them; it didn't.

Madson was closer to us now. I heard him say, "Have a seat on the couch. I'll go check on the girls and then we can go over the rules."

Princess said, "Sounds good."

Madson walked into the bedroom and the arrest team walked out. The team identified themselves calmly as law enforcement. They gave clear and concise commands. This works better than yelling at someone to comply. It also helped set the stage for my interview. Princess listened to the commands and was arrested without incident. Ted and I stayed in the bedroom until the arrest team advised that Princess had been searched for weapons.

Ted was my number two for the interview. I put my smile on as I walked out of the bedroom to introduce myself. That day I was wearing blue jeans, a blue flannel with brown and black accents, my favorite high-top Vans, and a beanie. I like to wear blue during interviews since it's a calming color.

Princess was seated on the sofa in handcuffs. I moved a chair closer to her and sat down. The sweat was beading up on her face as if she was a car with a fresh coat of wax on a rainy day.

The arrest team left, but Madson decided to stay. I thought, *Why is he staying here?* This was not ideal. Thing is, Madson had opened the door, invited her in, and then she was arrested. In her mind he was the reason she was in handcuffs. The fact that he was in the room could fuck up my interview.

I asked her, "Are you okay?"

She said, "This is a lot."

She looked like she was going to pop. I grabbed a trash can and placed it near her feet. She was wearing these *Little House on the Prairie* boots that came up just over her ankles. I motioned to Ted to get her some water.

"If I take your cuffs off, are you going to try anything crazy?"

She said, "No, please do."

I removed her handcuffs, and Ted gave her the water. She emptied the glass quickly. She pointed at the trash can.

"Can I move this closer?"

She didn't wait for me to answer and picked it up.

I answered anyway, "Of course you can."

Princess sat with arms crossed and her body slumped on the sofa. I explained I needed to advise her of her rights before I asked her any questions. After I was done, she agreed to speak with me.

Princess calmed down as we continued to talk. She quit sweating and her face gained some color back. Man, I thought for sure she was going to pop. I'm pretty good at getting it right, but this time I was wrong.

12

"We have been investigating a dad that is sex-trafficking his two little girls. We arrested him and assumed his identity. When you asked for a photo of the dad, we already had his phone."

Of course this was not what had happened, but I wanted her to believe the kids were real. She believed me.

The purpose of the interview was to gather evidence for the crimes of commercial sexual abuse of a minor, attempted rape of a child 1, attempted rape of a child 2, and promoting prostitution.

The commercial sexual abuse of a minor is just as it sounds. It is trading anything of value in exchange for a sex act with a minor.

The attempt rape of a child (AROC) 1 and 2 depends on the age of the minor. AROC1 means the minors are eleven years of age and younger. AROC2 means the minors are twelve or thirteen years of age.

The promoting prostitution is as it sounds.

As we talked with each other, she kept looking over at Madson. He was across from her leaning against a wall.

I said, "I know this isn't the most comfortable situation for you. If you are uncomfortable because someone is in the room, I can have them leave."

She looked at Madson and then back at me. I nodded and said, "Do you want him to leave? It's okay if you want him to go."

I looked at Madson while speaking to Princess and said, "He won't mind at all."

Madson did mind, but he got up and left. He minded because he wanted to hear what she had to say, not because his feelings were hurt. I could have told Madson to leave without asking Princess, but I wanted her to feel she had some say in what was happening, some control. Based on what the CI had told us and our chat conversation, I believed Princess enjoyed controlling others.

Once Madson was gone, Princess and I continued to talk. She told me about her family and how she was raised. As you can imagine, her experiences as a child were not ideal. Growing up, her father and his friends raped her one to two times a week up until she was eight years old. It would have continued, but she moved to another city with her mom and little sister. No dad.

Even though Princess wanted to have two little girls drugged so she could have sex with them, I felt sorry for her. I'm not saying it excuses her conduct, because it doesn't. In my experience just because a person is abused sexually doesn't mean they will become a sexual abuser. She made the choice to seek out someone who would drug their kids and let someone do the unthinkable. Even so, it still made me sad.

Next, Princess told me she was willing to try anything once and that is why she showed up.

"When you say you like to try everything once, what things have you tried?"

"These are like sexual things like BDSM, anal sex. More like master/slave stuff."

BDSM is a term used to describe sex that involves bondage,

dominance, submission, and control. The practice typically involves one partner taking on a more dominant role during sex, while the other is more submissive.

I said, "Okay."

"I mean, I still wanted to come, and obviously I am here right now. I brought lube." She described how her whole life, she didn't have a say in anything. "It's definitely a control thing."

"It is?"

"Yeah, cuz I'm not sexually attracted to children, but yeah, I think it is a control thing."

The words flowed so easily out of her mouth. I wish I could tell you I am the Michael Jordan of interviewing, but I am not. Sometimes they just let it flow. I don't know if it's because they are finally confessing, or it gets them off as they talk about it. It didn't matter; I went with it.

"So, you like being able to have control over something?"

"Yeah, cuz really, right now my life is just . . . out of control."

I have been trained to ask people what their fantasy is. Oftentimes it is something they have done or are wanting to become reality. Princess wanted to have sex with little girls while they were drugged. I wanted to know if this was the first time she had done this or if there were other victims.

Sometimes I come right out and ask what a person's fantasy is, and other times I frame the question in a different way.

"How did you envision everything happening?"

"Well, I was hoping I'd come in and kind of get to know this dude a little bit"—she motioned to where Madson had been in the room—"and then, you know, see if the girls were awake or sleeping or whatever . . . and if they were okay . . . maybe I would go in and, you know, kiss them a little bit."

Her tongue slipped out of her mouth and painted her lips with a fresh coat of saliva. She rubbed her lips together and then touched the corners of her mouth—one side with her index finger and the other side with her thumb. She brought her finger and thumb together along her bottom lip until they finally touched. She was thinking about it. She was imagining kissing the girls.

Princess was minimizing what she wanted to do with the girls, but at least she was talking with me.

I read her a portion of the text conversation.

"He texted you, 'Do you still want them sleeping? How much do you have?' And you said, 'I have $200 cash on me. I want them sleeping. Not awake. Too sketchy.' So, you didn't want them awake at all? Is that because you were afraid they would remember who you were?"

She said, "I don't want them to know what's going on cuz I don't want them to get messed up."

I wanted to believe her, but I did not.

13

When Princess walked into the room, she had a personal bag and a grocery bag. The grocery bag held a family-sized bag of Cool Ranch Doritos, a bottle of soda, sour cream, and lube. I asked Princess if I could search through her other bags. She said yes.

I asked Ted for some gloves to search the bags. I'd forgotten to replace the extra set I kept in my ballistic vest, and I didn't have any with me since I'd ridden with Ted.

Not one single person had gloves for me to use.

Shit. I didn't want to search her bags without gloves. Princess had told me she was bringing sex toys for the girls. I didn't want to touch her sex toys *with* gloves, so there was no way I was going to touch them *without* gloves. Who knew where those toys had been?

I was about to call for someone to drop some gloves off at our location when I noticed an ice bucket with a plastic bag on the hotel countertop. That poor bag would never get to hold ice.

I began to pull items out of her bag. The first item was a curved glass dildo about seven inches in length. The next was a set of pink silicone anal beads about ten inches long.

She said, "NOW! Just a reminder! Everything in that bag was not for them. It was just one thing and one thing only, otherwise I would have mentioned them in the texts."

"So just the glass dildo?"

"Yes."

Okay, just a seven-inch glass dildo for two little kids. No problem. That made it all better.

I continued my search and removed the following items:

- One large penis-shaped dildo

- One butt plug

- A speculum

- One large glass penis-shaped dildo about twelve inches in length

- Some clamps for her breasts that she called "tit things."

You know, all the fun toys that kids ask Santa for.

14

After searching the bag, I sat back down.

"Why are you here?"

She stared at the floor while she chewed on the nail of her index finger. After a few nibbles she moved on to the nail of her middle finger. She said nothing. We sat in the silence. I looked at Ted and nodded to him.

Finally, she whispered, "I told you why I'm here."

I didn't speak. I let her sit in the moment. I watched her and waited.

She continued, "You know, I wanna . . ."

She looked up at me and then placed one hand just beneath her chin. She slid her fingers down toward her chest. When she reached her chest, she placed the same hand just below her chin and started again. She repeated this several times.

Princess said, "You know, I came in and I thought . . . I could provide oral to the girls. You know, have sex like I said before; that was my plan."

"So, your plan was to have sex with the girls first and then try to have sex with him after?"

Her fingers continued to trail down her neck. She said, "Have oral sex with the girls."

"So, you wanted oral with the girls?"

"Mm-hmm."

"And oral to you, that's?"

"That's me kissing their labia."

I asked her to describe what she thought oral was because the definition mattered in how she would be charged.

She said, "Well, I just wanted the labia really, the clit. That's more of what I was going for."

I asked, "And then fingers, and then maybe the glass dildo?"

"Maybe. Yeah."

"But that's what you guys had agreed to and what you were paying for?"

"Mm-hmm."

"Is that because you feel sad?"

I asked this question because I had prior knowledge there were videos and images of her harming small animals. This in itself is sad. Even so, a person that is a sadist or derives pleasure from these types of images is not sad. This excites them. I wanted to see what Princess would say and then adjust my questioning from there.

Princess nodded yes to me. She was sitting "crisscross, applesauce" like a child on the couch now. She stopped stroking her neck.

I told her I believed she was sad based on what she had told me and from my experience doing my job. She lowered her head. I told her I thought she liked the power and control and the sad part of it.

I asked, "Have you ever hurt any animals?"

Princess quickly lifted her head. "No."

"Never?"

"Never."

"You've never talked about it?"

She shook her head no. I turned my head to the side and opened my hands like Tim Robinson when he says, "You sure 'bout that?"

I said, "You hesitated."

She shook her head no more quickly, as if that would convince me.

"You have never talked about hurting animals. Ever."

Again, with the quick head shake.

"So, we are not going to see any of that on your phone?"

Princess didn't nod this time. She locked eyes with me but was motionless.

I maintained eye contact with her and said, "I think you have. I think some of that is going to be on your phone, talking about some of that type of stuff. I think some of it is going to be more sadistic-type things."

She nibbled on her thumb this time.

"Dealing with pain and misery. Just from talking with you."

She stopped nibbling and transitioned to stroking her neck again.

I asked, "Am I wrong?"

I knew I was right. Still, I wanted her to tell me. I wanted her to admit it.

A three-second sigh escaped her mouth.

"Will you do me a favor, if you can?"

Princess changed the subject and asked for a phone number from her phone. I told her no. I asked the question again. She told me to move on.

"Is it because you don't like hearing it out loud or is it because you think you might get in more trouble?"

"It could be both . . . I don't trust you guys, but there is texting about possibly . . . snake . . . mice."

"Okay."

"I'm not sexually attracted to children. I just wanted a situation that I could be in control. Whether this situation or whether you were texting me about, you know, an animal. Regardless of the situation, whatever you would have texted me about, I feel like I would have been open to maybe possibly doing it."

She was so calm as she explained herself.

She continued, "I had no plans on, you know, hurting them, the girls, at all. I just wanted to give them kisses and love on them, and then leave."

I gripped my right hand with my left, squeezing as hard as I could.

Breathe. Settle. Focus. I hoped my face didn't deceive me and show my disgust. I continued to listen.

She said again, "It might be a control thing."

She let out another sigh, this one shorter.

"I know you can't tell me how long, but I am so concerned about how long I'm going to be in prison for."

At the end of our conversation, I asked Princess if there was anything else she wanted to add.

She said, "I mean . . . really? What happens to girls that you see come through here? Do they ever get out?"

"Do you mean the ones that I have arrested or the ones that we rescued?"

I knew she was asking about herself.

She said, "The ones you arrest."

"Well, every situation is different. All the ones I know of are still in prison."

She whispered, "Goddamn it."

"So, you are talking about yourself and not the girls."

"No, I am glad they are safe."

I said nothing.

"I just . . . Do you think I deserve it?"

I did not answer her question.

15

"Do you think I deserve it?"

I still think about this question. At the time of the interview, I absolutely thought she deserved it. I wanted her in prison for the rest of her life.

Now? Do I think she deserved it? Did she deserve being raped by her father and his friends? Absolutely not. Did she deserve all the other horrible things that happened to her that she did not share with me? No. She did not.

Did that excuse her from wanting to have two little kids drugged so she could have her way with them? Of course not. She made that choice. That was her decision.

Princess pled guilty to attempted rape of a child in the first degree, commercial sexual abuse of a minor, and promoting prostitution. She was sentenced to just over eight years with a chance to serve life in prison.

This is all so tragic.

Some may say there are no winners here. I disagree. We made sure one less person had the opportunity to harm a kid, and Princess is in a facility where she can get some services to work through some of her inner demons if she chooses to. Will that stop her desires? I don't think so, but I don't have that answer. Is our community safer by her being in prison? Yes, I believe it is, and that, my friends, is a win.

SIXTEEN

THE LETTER

1

My phone rang. "Sergeant Rodriguez."

I was greeted with a slow "Yo."

It was my friend Shaw. He was working for Washington State's Office of the Attorney General and was Washington state's human trafficking coordinator. I first met him when he was a Kitsap County deputy prosecutor, and I was at WestNET.

Through the years we kept in touch. When I was at MECTF, Shaw asked me to do training with him and a group of other child exploitation and human trafficking subject matter experts. We provided training throughout Washington state.

Shaw is passionate about protecting the rights of others, especially vulnerable persons. Shaw always knows what to say. Being around him makes me feel more confident in my own decisions.

"I have this group you should meet," said Shaw. "They are pretty chill and doing some great things for trafficked persons. They could benefit from meeting you. It could be really good."

Shaw enjoys connecting people. He wanted me to meet this group and talk about the operations MECTF was conducting around the state. My command staff approved the meeting, and I put together a sanitized presentation suitable for a public group.

What I mean by sanitized is a PG version of the work my task force conducted. It didn't reveal the identities of any exploited persons or disclose any law enforcement tactics that could jeopardize future operations.

The nonprofit is called Stolen Youth. They raise funds and invest in organizations working to dismantle the marketplace exploiting children for sex. Shaw and I met with one of the founders. I shared with her the work my small task force did around Washington state.

As I explained how easy it was for people to seek out children for sex on the internet, she began to cry. I was only about ten minutes into the presentation. I stopped talking.

I felt horrible making this nice woman cry. She told me to continue. I wondered if my presentation wasn't sanitized enough. When I'd edited the presentation, I thought I was careful not to leave anything too shocking in. Was it too much?

After the presentation I spoke with Shaw. "How was it? I thought I'd sanitized it pretty well."

He said, "Yeah, man, that was intense."

"I mean, if I took any more out of the presentation it would be hard to grasp what we are trying to prevent."

He said, "That's not it. We are in it every day. We can become a little desensitized to how bad this shit is."

Her reaction was the correct reaction. Even though I was not going into detail, the mere fact of an adult seeking to have sex with children is jarring. This was painful to hear. The amount of people seeking to have sex with children is shocking.

In my world, it was commonplace for people to damage kids over and over. It still impacted me negatively, but I was able to shut parts of me off. Seeing the Ugly day in and day out had altered my norm.

2

A few months later, Stolen Youth asked me to present at their yearly luncheon. They asked if I would share the story of a trafficked person from one of my cases.

I kindly told them, "I can't do that. Thank you, but that is not my story to tell. However, I can share how working these cases has changed me, as well as my perspective as an investigator."

They agreed that it wasn't my place to tell the story of an exploited person, and it would be wonderful if I could be a part of the luncheon.

This was new to me. I had never done anything like this before. As the luncheon approached, I learned there would be about one thousand people in attendance. The audience included local celebrities, philanthropists, and politicians.

I was nervous, but then I thought, *If someone else has done it, then I know I can.*

I asked Stolen Youth if my detectives could attend. They were excited about the idea of my team attending. They provided a table for us. I didn't want my team there to watch me speak. It wasn't that at all. I wanted them to see people care about what they were fighting for. I wanted them to know people appreciated what they do.

Law enforcement as a whole doesn't get enough recognition for what they do. Oftentimes it is a thankless job. I'm not saying my detectives asked for recognition. It's the exact opposite. I can't think of one time they wanted or asked to be recognized for their work.

Even so, it was important to me. I wanted them to know what they did mattered to others outside of our office.

3

I completed my speech a few weeks before the luncheon. I asked Julie if she would listen to me read it and give me some feedback. We were in our kitchen, and Liv overheard me ask her mom. She said, "Dad, I want to hear it too."

Liv was sixteen years old, and she knew what I did for work now. She knew it was difficult and I saw terrible things. Although she knew what I did, she did not know everything. That was on purpose. My family didn't need to know all the dark details. That was for me to manage, not them. My family was my safe space, my escape from the Ugly.

Julie nodded that it would be okay.

Liv and I sat down at our kitchen table. Julie stood next to me. I removed a paper square from my back pocket, unfolded it, and placed it on the table in front of me. After pausing for a few seconds, I began.

4

Hello, I am Carlos Rodriguez, and I am a sergeant with the Washington State Patrol's Missing and Exploited Children Task Force, MECTF. I started with the WSP in 1993 and have been with the task force for about five years.

Today I am here for several reasons.

I am here to express how real the threat is to our children and how you can help keep them safe.

The cases my task force investigates involve people carrying out horrible acts on the most innocent members of our community, our children.

We are tasked with investigating all crimes against children. Unfortunately, the majority of these crimes involve sexually exploiting our kids.

- *Paying for sex with children*

- *Molesting children*

- *Raping children*

- *Documenting and distributing these acts with photos and videos*

These are all big problems, real problems.

Several years ago, I asked myself, How do we get ahead of these problems? *Today I want to share with you a proactive approach to preventing sex crimes against children. Using this approach, we rescue children and catch those that prey on our children.*

Let me tell you my task force is small—two, sometimes three of us total, and our area of responsibility is the entire state of Washington. This responsibility is overwhelming. At times it seems impossible.

To be effective, we have become great at making friends with other task forces and law enforcement agencies. Without their help, we simply could not function.

My task force and I go where these predators search for our kids. We conduct undercover operations posing as adults providing children for sex acts. We also pose as vulnerable children.

When I say children, I don't mean just teenagers.

I mean kids.

Ages eleven,

ten,

six,

five.

Children.

We began conducting these operations in Kitsap County in August of 2015. As of today, we have conducted seven operations in Washington state. The operations take about two weeks to set up and last for about four days, with a few follow-up arrests.

In the last eighteen months, my small task force has arrested a total of eighty-six people.

More importantly, we have rescued twenty-one children.

I know we have rescued more because we are removing these predators from our community.

Before we met these predators, they had access to at least 110 children that we know of.

We have conducted these operations across the state and, unfortunately, the demand for this is alive and well everywhere we go.

People ask me, "How can you do your job?"

I am a parent. I am a person just like you.

I tell them there is nothing more important than a child. If I don't do this, who will?

When I get the opportunity to interview a suspect, I tell them, "I am glad I met you. I am glad it was me waiting for you instead of the six-year-old you showed up to meet."

I call it an opportunity because it means I have a chance to save a child.

We can stop children from being hurt.

The hardest part of our job is not meeting with those that hurt children.

The hardest part is seeing the damage they have done.

I have listened to horrible things, things no matter how much I try to forget, I simply can't.

My voice began to waver. This was more difficult than I thought.

It is hard to listen to a twelve-year-old little girl describe how she and her sister were raped and assaulted. I listened as tears rolled down her face. This tiny little girl was not more than sixty pounds.

She detailed violent, horrific things that should never happen to any-one, especially not to her. Especially not to her sister.

I paused again to gather myself. I looked at my Liv. Her face told me she was worried about me.

I took a long breath in. My throat was tight. It hurt to swallow. I wanted some water.

I have recovered young girls from hotel rooms that were sex-trafficked time and time again. I remember looking at one in particular just before this past New Year.

What is difficult for me is how much she reminds me of my own daughter.

Not her actions. Not what she is going through, but the fact she is the same age as my daughter. It makes me think, That could be my little girl.

I could hear my daughter and Julie both sniffling. I did not look up at them; otherwise, I wasn't sure if I would be able to continue. Julie placed her hand on my shoulder.

I remember how I wanted her to be whole again and not live the life she was living. I listened to her mother describe the agony she went through when her child was being sex-trafficked and how helpless she felt.

I still wish I could have done more to help her and her daughter.

When you see this on the news, it seems so surreal because there are no names attached.

They say: Juvenile victim or a minor.

You don't hear their names.

Names like:

Cristal

Samantha

Lucas

Ted

Natalie

They have names.

The names I just listed are not children.

They are the names of those I work with.

They are my friends, and I am proud of them.

The point I want to make is this: When you hear a name, when you know the name, it is so real. This is real.

All of this is uncomfortable to hear. It hurts to listen to it, but I know the discomfort I am experiencing is nothing compared to the pain I just described to you.

Their pain drives me and those I work with to do more.

When I say that I always make it a point to say it with a smile, I do that because this is dark, and we all need to smile more.

We need to do more.

We need a shift in priorities to keep our children safe.

After I tell people why I do this, they usually tell me thank you. Sometimes they give me a hug. Most ask me how they can help me. They say, "What can I do to support your efforts?"

First, I tell them, get involved. Be a good parent. Take the time to get to know your kids' friends and their parents. Know what your kids are doing. Be present.

If something doesn't seem right, most likely it isn't. Love your kids and give them the confidence to make the right decisions.

Next, I say, support what we do. Tell your community about my task force and that you support our efforts. My task force has the unique ability to receive public and private grants and gifts. This allows my task force to work with groups like Stolen Youth.

The job I do is difficult, to say the least, but as I look at those of you here today, I am energized.

Moments like this are so important. Together we can make an impact. I know we can.

I could talk all day about what my task force does and what our needs are, but today is about supporting Stolen Youth. Thank you for listening. With your support, we can do so much more.

I placed the pages onto the table in front of me. My chair legs scraped across the tiled kitchen floor as I pushed myself away from the table. I wrapped my arms around Liv, and we cried together.

The last time Liv had seen me cry was when I learned my friend Ronnie was murdered. This was a different cry, though. It was more of a pressure release. I was sad and happy at the same time. I was sad Liv was crying but happy she was hugging me.

Sharing my experiences by reading that speech to Julie and my daughter left me feeling vulnerable. I didn't realize that sharing how I felt working these cases would cause me to react that way. It was weird to see it on paper and even weirder to read it out loud. I didn't like not being in control of how I felt.

5

A few weeks later I presented at the luncheon. As I walked onto the stage, I hoped I would keep it together. Once at the podium, my nerves settled. I couldn't see the nearly thousand people in the room any longer. Only bright orbs of the light surrounded by darkness. I could hear voices murmuring softly and the silverware clinking against ceramic plates as the attendees ate their lunch.

As I shared a bit of my world with a room full of strangers, the murmur diminished and the clinking faded. By the middle of my speech, the room was silent. The room felt empty. The silence lasted a few seconds after my last word and was replaced with applause. I walked off the stage and sat at my table.

One less box.

SEVENTEEN

"DON'T LET ME FAIL."

1

Throughout my life I have spent a lot of time managing one traumatic incident after another. I shared with you how I shut parts of myself down mentally to survive and operate in the Ugly.

What was unpredictable for most became predictable for me. I planned for most things, realizing I didn't have control over much I was faced with. I worked proactive operations attempting to get some control back, to get ahead of the damage done to kids and their families.

The intention of my team and me was to protect children from harm and hold those intending to do harm to kids accountable.

I know when I base my actions on my intentions, I have a better chance of getting the outcome I want. This was no different.

My parents raised me to work hard and to do my best to help others. I believe that is why I gravitated toward a life of service. The traumatic things that happened in my life granted me a unique skill set to thrive in chaotic situations, a way to organize the chaos.

There were days I told myself, *I can't go in. Don't get up. Go back to sleep. I don't want to do this today. This isn't sustainable.*

Did I want to quit? Yes. Just like I wanted to quit the first night in the academy. Back then it was David's white shoe in the roadway that prompted me to ask, "Who do I want to be?"

Working these cases, it wasn't about who I wanted to be. It was more about what would happen if I was not this person.

There were many reasons why I thought of quitting:

- Watching a parent crumble from the weight of my words as I told them what happened to their baby

- Remembering my detectives telling me, "I'm good," and knowing they were not

- Never finding the little boy who sent a selfie of himself posing in front of a bathroom mirror to a suspect's phone

Funny thing is, these same things were the reasons why I did not quit.

2

When I neared retirement, I sat down with my lieutenant at the time, James Mjor. You are thinking, *How do I say that?* It's pronounced Me-Your, not May-Jur.

James wasn't just my lieutenant; he was and still is my friend. James is a former Navy SEAL. You wouldn't know it from him telling you, though. That's how he is built—humble. James does have a lot of nicknames, though.

When someone has a lot of nicknames, it means they are loved.

Some call him Shooter, some Cecil, and some call him Jimmy Time. I call him brother.

Close your eyes and imagine a Navy SEAL. If you need some help, imagine the scene in the movie *The Rock* when the team is going through the tunnels into Alcatraz, or *Zero Dark Thirty* when they take out Bin Ladin. Bad-ass motherfuckers. Got it? Now scrap that.

James looks nothing like those dudes.

He has red hair, is stocky, and five-seven or five-eight depending on what shoes he wears.

James is like a French bulldog—gentle, kid-friendly, loyal, and kind of gassy. Frenchies are known for their affectionate nature but can be aggressive. That's James—kind, but he can flip the switch when needed.

James and I discussed what was going to happen when I retired. We talked about a plan to ensure the task force continued to grow and do great work. We knew if we didn't plan now, it would be too late when I left, and the task force would suffer for it. Our community would suffer for it. That wasn't an option. After our meeting I met with my team and included HTCU.

I told them I planned on retiring in two years and I needed their help with an exit plan.

One detective said, "You aren't leaving in two years, Sarge. You're never going to stop doing this."

I asked him, "What happens if I die tomorrow?"

He quit smiling. The room went quiet.

I asked the team as a whole, "What happens if one of you leaves? What is your plan? What is our plan?"

In that moment as I looked at their faces, I missed them. I realized I would not be doing this forever and I would miss it, I would miss them. I don't know if you can understand that or not, but that's how I felt.

We talked about how we all had our own unique skill sets. I asked each of them to do more. What we were fighting for deserved that we do more.

From that point forward I expected my team to become proficient in the areas of the operation that they were not familiar with. I said, "Each of you will rotate through different team leader positions so you know what to do. I won't be the only person planning the operations any longer. We will share that responsibility."

We discussed how we would start to identify potential replacements for the team so when they left, the work would continue.

I said, "If this ceases to exist when I am gone, I have failed. If this ceases to exist when you are gone, we have failed. My success is determined by your success. Your success is determined by those sitting in this room with you. This is bigger than all of us. Don't let me fail."

EIGHTEEN

LOVE ITCHES

1

Like I mentioned already, I look younger than most for my age. As a teenager I swore someone had placed a voodoo curse on me. Dating girls was a bitch.

In addition to looking so young, I had a condition with my face called UGLY. My orthodontist called it an underbite. He told me my upper jaw did not grow as much as my lower jaw. My face looked like a shallow plate with a nose in the middle of it. I had no cheekbones. Just eyes, nose, and a mouth.

When I graduated from high school, I underwent surgery to correct my bite. During the surgery they peeled my face back, sawed through my upper jaw, and corrected my bite. When the swelling subsided, my plate face was gone, and girls started to pay attention to me. Even so, I still looked twelve when I was nineteen.

All through my teenage years and up until I was twenty-one, I never wanted a girlfriend. Yes. I wanted to be with girls. I wanted to be with girls in all the ways boys want to be with girls. I just didn't want to be committed to any one girl.

I was honest about it.

I would tell the girl I was interested in, "I don't want to be your boyfriend. I like you and want to spend time with you, but no on the boyfriend."

I didn't have sex until I was nearly nineteen. It was technically sex, but I had no idea what I was doing. It was quick and I was petrified. I had upgraded from the 1985 Prelude to a white 1990 Honda Prelude. My first time having sex was in the front passenger seat of that Honda with a cheerleader.

My friends used to call her "Bird" because she was so skinny. I remember her hair being so thick she cut her hair short only on the back of her head so her hair would lie down correctly. At least that's why I thought she did it. I didn't care. She was cute and extremely intelligent. More importantly, she liked me, even with my plate face. She was popular and I was not. It was a win for me.

We did not use a condom. I was terrified afterward. You see, I knew nothing about sex. I knew where "it" went and that if you didn't use a condom, you would catch a disease. That's what I was taught. No condom means you get a disease and will die.

Afterward I drove directly to the emergency room at Madigan Hospital located on JBLM. I checked myself in.

The nurse asked, "What do you need to be seen for?" or something like that.

I said, "Um, I am here because I itch."

She asked, "Okay? Where do you itch?"

I said, "Down there."

She said, "Oh, okay. Are you sexually active?"

"Yes, ma'am."

"How long have you been sexually active?"

"Um, tonight."

She bit her bottom lip, trying to swallow her smile. She failed. The nurse took a moment to gather herself and then continued to check me in. Shortly thereafter, two doctors came in and began to ask me questions.

"Carlos, I understand you are experiencing some, let's see here . . . itching."

"Yes, sir . . . um, down there."

"And you had sex tonight for the first time?"

"Yes, sir."

The doctors were across from me, smiling a little while asking me doctor questions. They had me remove my pants and underwear. They conducted an exam and advised me they thought I was going to be okay, but I should use protection. I left feeling embarrassed, but also relieved. I was going to live.

2

I didn't see the cheerleader any longer. I remember her telling me it was okay and that she knew I was just curious. That was the first of many extremely short relationships that were just about sex.

Then I met Julie, my future wife.

Julie was different. She knew what she wanted and taught me it was okay to love her. She also set boundaries.

One was that she refused to meet my dad unless she was my girlfriend. She felt if our relationship wasn't going anywhere, why should she meet my dad? She was right, and I did want her to meet my dad.

I did want her to be my girlfriend. I tried to play it cool like I didn't want her to be my girlfriend.

I said, "Okay, fine. You are my girlfriend."

She said, "No. No, I'm not. Not like that. I'm serious."

I was such an idiot.

Julie is two inches shorter than me. When she walked into a room, she collected eyes like a magnet attracts metal. When she smiled, I felt happy. She has these deep dimples, one side deeper than the other, but it's a good look. When we met, she had long, curly blonde hair and big brown eyes. People stopped her frequently and said, "Has anybody ever told you that you look like Kelly Ripa?"

Julie was mature for her age, strong-willed, and spoke her mind. I think it was because she grew up without her father, Don.

Don passed from kidney cancer when Julie was nine years old, the same age I was when my grandma last hugged me. Don was a Green Beret and served in the Vietnam War. His family believed he got his cancer from Agent Orange.

I never met Don, but I did listen to audiotapes of him playing with Julie and her brothers. He had a soft, comforting voice. I could hear the love he had for his family as he sang "There Was an Old Lady Who Swallowed a Fly."

Julie told me stories about how her dad would get on all fours, and she and her brothers would ride on his back. When I saw photos of him, he looked back with kind eyes. Julie has the same kind eyes.

I didn't want Julie to leave me, so I started over and shared how I felt about her. I asked her to be my girlfriend, and she said yes.

We drove to my dad's, and of course he loved her. My dad pulled me aside and said, "Son, that's the one."

He was right. Julie and I got married on August 3, 1996, and we were married for twenty-five years.

NINETEEN

SAME DRIVE, DIFFERENT DRIVER

1

I had just returned home from a work trip. I was three months into my retirement from the WSP, but I never really retired. I took a break for about a month and then started to work for a nonprofit organization.

Julie and I were supposed to travel to Clearwater, Florida, for a work conference two days later. My new profession required me to travel frequently. I thought this was great since Julie wanted to travel the world with me.

When I worked for the WSP, I told her, "When I retire, we will travel."

She said, "I want to see Italy."

"We will! When I retire. I promise."

Before I retired, we did travel, but mostly to the same places. We went to Mexico and Disney World for most family vacations, but Disney World's EPCOT World Showcase isn't what Julie meant by seeing the world. After I retired, Covid happened, and that cancelled Italy.

2

When I got home, I pet our corgis Mando and Millie, said hi to the kids, and then hugged Julie. She wanted to speak with me up in our bedroom.

I said, "Everything good?"

She said, "Let's go upstairs."

That wasn't good. I thought something must be wrong with one of the kids. I followed her up the stairs and into our bedroom. Just before I walked into our room, I could smell lavender Fabuloso. The room looked like it had been prepped for a photo session. Julie drinks water like a fish and had a habit of leaving empty water glasses on her bedside table. They were gone. Her table looked naked without them. All the clutter in our room was missing.

The bed was dressed neatly with a white comforter and topped with several matching pillows. She cleaned like this when she was stressed. Something was definitely wrong.

"Wow! Honey, it looks nice in here."

She motioned for me to close the door. I turned around and grabbed the door handle. The crescent-shaped scrapes on the wood floor reminded me to pull up on the handle slightly as I pushed the door shut. Julie was standing next to her side of the bed, her arms at her side, her hands formed into fists.

When Julie makes a fist, she grips her thumb with her fingers instead of wrapping her thumb around her index finger. It always made me laugh. I used to tell her, "You will break your thumb if you punch someone that way."

She would say, "Oh yeah!" and then punch at me while laughing. She wasn't laughing today.

Julie took a deep breath and lifted her arms slightly. She exhaled and released her fingers. Band-Aids were wrapped around every one of her fingertips. When Julie was anxious, she picked at her fingertips. The Band-Aids were there to stop the picking. It didn't really work.

Julie said, "I can't get over it. I tried. I just can't. I want a divorce."

3

Two years earlier I had been at a conference. I chose to share an Uber ride home with another woman who had attended the conference. We made out on the way back to the hotel. Although we were both intoxicated, it does not excuse my choice. I cheated on Julie.

About a month later, I told Julie what I had done. It was horrible. I had betrayed her and my family. I told her what I did for several reasons. The main reason was the guilt of it. Yes, I didn't want to lose her, but I also was worried she would find out. I was selfish. I wanted to dump the weight of it.

Over the next couple of years, we tried to work on our relationship, but it did not work. I thought we were on a good path, but I was so wrong. I was not present.

Like I shared before, when I was present physically, I was not available for her emotionally or mentally. If I had been, I would have seen this coming. The truth is, I did not invest in our relationship. My choice reflected that. I failed us. I failed my family. I hurt the person that cared for me the most.

I had smashed our teacup and there wasn't enough glue to put it back together.

I believe life is a series of choices. Good or bad, the choices we make determine what happens in our lives. The choices I made cost me my best friend.

4

The worst part of all of this was what I put our kids through. We decided to tell Liv and Noah two weeks later after I came back from a couple of out-of-state work trips. We called them up to our bedroom. Julie and I stood next to her side of the bed and faced the door. I could hear them walking up the stairs. Julie and I were nervous.

She told me, "It will be all right."

Liv entered first followed by Noah. Liv was holding her arms at her side. She had the same fists as her mother minus the Band-Aids. They both stood there quietly and waited for us to speak. Julie and I looked at each other and then back at the kids. We told them we were ending our marriage.

Julie didn't want them to hate me, so we agreed to tell them we had made the choice together. She still cared about me even when I had hurt her.

Their bodies fell limp. It transported me back to my apartment in Oklahoma when I was seventeen. I had become my mother. I saw myself and my sister in my kids. Is this what my parents saw so many years ago?

Liv's face crinkled up. She covered her face when she realized she couldn't stop what was coming. Tears escaped through her fingers, soaking her shirt. Some made it to the floor.

She sobbed, "I knew this was going to happen."

I had failed my children. I had failed my wife. I had caused this.

Julie hugged Liv.

I shifted my attention to my son. He was taller, stronger, and bigger than me now. His eyes watered, but no tears fell. I saw myself. I watched him slowly shut off his emotions. His eyes dried. He was filling a box.

Liv wanted to be alone and quickly left. Julie followed her downstairs to comfort her. Noah stayed in the room with me. He opened his mouth, but no words came out. He closed his mouth and tried again.

"I kind of knew this was probably going to happen. I could kinda tell."

He was so calm.

"Don't worry, Dad. I will be okay. Liv will too. I will take care of her. She just needs some time."

A few tears salted my lips. "I'm so sorry, Noah."

"It's going to be okay, Dad."

Noah kept it together. At least while he was in the room with me.

"I need to go see E-Rob and then go drive for a while. He is waiting for me so I should go."

E-Rob is one of Noah's best friends. Noah hugged me and then left me alone in the room.

I waited for Julie to come back upstairs. She told me it would take some time, but they would be okay. That's what everybody says in those moments, right? We agreed to keep the process civil.

She told me, "The worst part of this is you are my best friend. I don't want to lose that."

I didn't either, but I knew I already had. Before I left, we hugged. I didn't want to let go of her. I feared this would be the last time we would embrace. After a few seconds her body tensed up. We let go of each other. I felt cold. I walked downstairs, went out to my car, and left for a drive. No Judson Spence this time. Just my thoughts.

5

It's easy for me to blame my cheating on my job, but that isn't the truth. I know I lost the ability to feel certain things. Yes, that did make it easier for me to be unfaithful, but that doesn't excuse the choice I made. That is on me.

Julie and my kids deserved better, just like my dad and my sister deserved better. I did what my mom did to my family growing up. I did to my family what I was trying to keep from happening to me. How embarrassing. Then I thought of my sister.

When my parents told Carmen and me they were getting a divorce, I didn't think about how she felt. My sister was only eleven years old, and I left her alone. I never gave it a thought until thirty-two years later when Julie and I told our kids we were doing the same thing.

Why didn't I react like my son? He thought of everyone else but himself. I had thought of only myself. I called my sister and told her what had happened.

I love my sister, even though my actions say I am not the best brother. I don't talk to her regularly. For a long time, I didn't answer her texts or return her calls right away. Again, selfish.

Our relationship was not always that way. I believe people that are selfless in some areas of their lives can be selfish in others if they are not careful. I allowed my work to consume me. I gave so much of myself to others, and those closest to me suffered for it. I regret that.

Carmen was forty-four years old when I called her. I apologized for leaving her so many years ago. I told her I was just a kid, but I should have protected her.

"I'm sorry I left you. I am sorry for not being a good brother."

Carmen did what she always did. She tried to make me feel better.

She told me it was okay and that she didn't even remember me leaving. She told me I was a great brother to her and a great father to my kids. She told me to take the time to grieve and that everything would be okay.

Then she said, "I know you don't believe the same way I do, but is it okay if I pray for you?"

I said, "Yes, I don't mind."

We said we loved each other and then hung up.

6

I have read this chapter many times to myself. Different thoughts and feelings come to me. After reading it several times, I felt the need to call my mom. I was afraid, but I did it anyway.

"Hi Mijo, I'm so glad you called. Is everything okay?"

She always asks me that because I don't call her much. I told her I was writing this book, and I needed to talk to her about it before it was published.

"The book is about my work and how the experiences in my life prepared me for what I was able to do in a weird way. Some of those things affected me negatively. I want you to know some of those things are things you did."

No sound came from her end of the phone.

"I don't want you to think I'm painting you poorly. I'm not. I am the person I am today because of you and Dad. I have a lot of great qualities because of you."

I paused for a few seconds.

"I know now that our kids don't understand why parents make the decisions they do, and I don't need to know why you made the decisions you made. It doesn't matter. What matters is how I perceived it.

When you cheated on Dad with that man, Lewis, it made me angry with you."

She said, "I know."

"I am still angry."

I paused again to swallow.

"After that I never wanted a girlfriend, fearing that would happen to me. I still have a problem with that."

My voice was shaking now.

"Mom, what sucks is . . . what sucks is I was trying to avoid that happening to me, but I did the same thing to Julie and the kids. I'm . . ."

I had to stop to gather myself. The words were there, but I couldn't get them out of my mouth. I wiped tears from my cheeks.

"I'm not saying it's your fault. It's mine. My choices led to that. I also want you to know I don't hate you. I love you. I know you did the best you knew how and that you love me. I'm sorry I'm not the best son, it's just . . . I'm still angry."

She said nothing.

I said, "I'm working on it. I'm working on our teacup still."

The conversation slowly changed to my mom wanting the best for me and how everything she did was with good intentions. Shortly after that we said goodbye.

RIVER

1

Writing all of this reminds me of something RTBB shared with me. This was before I was introduced to the Ugly. I was having a problem with a supervisor from another agency that we called the Pearl. I met with RTBB for some guidance. Randy said, "I want you to try something. Just play along."

I said, "Okay."

He made a fist with one hand and held it up in front of him.

"This, right here."

He shook his fist like a boxer posing at a press event.

"It's a big-ass boulder. An immoveable object. It ain't going anywhere."

He opened his other hand and pressed his fingers together as if he'd shot paper in a game of rock, paper, scissors. His arm was parallel to the ground in front of him. He moved it up and down slightly and said, "Now this. This is you."

His arm slithered side to side like a snake.

"You . . . are a river."

His hand slithered up to the boulder and stopped.

"Los, what does a river do when it meets a boulder?"

I said, "Um, it goes around it?"

"Fucking right it does. Can you stop a river?"

"No. No, you can't."

He said, "A river always finds its way to its destination. You are a river. You can't be stopped."

He pumped his fist up and down twice.

"What happens to this here boulder?"

I said, "It stays there?"

"Yes, it does, and over time, the river wears the boulder down until it ceases to exist."

Randy put his hands down to his sides.

"Whenever you have a problem, just remember you are a river. You will always get around it. You always have, Carlos. Don't forget that."

2

If you are doing this work, thank you.

Make friends. You can try to do it alone, but it's a lot more fun when you have friends to share the journey. The friends you make along the way need you as much as you need them.

Don't be discouraged when people see things differently than you. They may be the solution or the enhancement that you need. This is not easy. Keep an open mind and remember, "You are a river."

TWENTY-ONE

"YOU DON'T GET THESE DAYS BACK."

1

My team started having what we called wellness nights after we wrapped up our Net Nanny operations. We would get together at a local bar for some food, drinks, and good conversation. This was our way to enjoy time together without focusing on the Ugly. Well, at least not the entire time.

I don't remember what bar we were at the night this happened, but I do remember it was cozy and quiet enough for us to hear each other talk.

One of the sergeants called us together for a toast. I called him Heisenberg because he looks like Walter White from *Breaking Bad*—so much so that I bought him the same hat and he wore it from time to time.

I recruited Heisenberg to help us on the OPs because of his experience working undercover investigating organized crime organizations. He also trained law enforcement officers from across the nation as undercover operatives. Adding Heisenberg to our team was a no-brainer. I utilized him mainly to manage my undercover decoys and close cover teams.

There were about ten of us there that night. Most of us drank old-fashioneds then. Heisenberg raised his glass in the air and the rest of us followed suit. He didn't say anything and just held the glass there until everyone was quiet. Then he said, "You don't get these days back."

We all repeated after him, "You don't get these days back."

We started saying that every time we made a toast.

I love those words. They remind me to be present in the moment and to be thankful for what I was allowed to be a part of. When I was with my team on nights like this, we focused on each other and not the Ugly. We were living in that moment surrounded by positive people. I'm so grateful for that time.

It was easy for me to get lost in my responsibilities. As a task force supervisor, I had to be successful at managing many things all at once:

- Logistics for large-scale operations

- Investigating multiple cases and meeting multiple deadlines

- Traveling from city to city and state to state

- Ensuring the needs of others were met

If I failed, it was a disservice to my team, my community, and ultimately those that I was trying to protect.

Constantly juggling all those things made it hard to live in the moment.

"You don't get these days back."

Those words serve as a reminder to take a breath. To enjoy the moment. To focus on what matters and on what I can control in that moment, even if it's only a little bit.

2

After my time with the WSP, it takes a lot to stress me out or get me riled up. When I deal with problems now, it feels like everything is in slow motion and I'm moving in real time. The problems I deal with now are still important, but the urgency isn't on the same level.

Do I miss the dance? Absolutely. Yes, I do. I miss organizing the chaos. Just a little bit. I don't miss all of it, though. I don't miss the Ugly. I don't miss it because it still clings to me, the uncomfortable feeling of it. We are connected, and I'm not sure if I will ever shake that. I'm not sure if I ever want to.

In a weird way it serves as a reminder of why I sacrificed some of the things that I did. It's a puzzle I haven't solved yet, but that's okay. I like solving puzzles.

Am I happy? I am happy most days. I have good days and bad days. Like I used to say, "There is more cream than there is sour milk."

TWENTY-TWO

HOW CAN I HELP?

I get asked this question a lot. First off, I say educate yourself. A great way to do this is by visiting the NCMEC at missingkids.org. It is a trusted website with real information. This will help you stay away from conspiracy theories and false narratives.

If you live in Washington state, call your state representatives, call your governor, and call the office of the chief for the WSP to tell them you want funding dedicated to an MECTF in your community.

No matter where you live, child trafficking and abuse is happening in your community. Call your elected officials and tell them you want resources dedicated to stopping this.

Connect with organizations like RAVEN.

RAVEN exists to transform our nation's response to child exploitation. They are the first and only 501(c)(4) group focused on child exploitation in the United States. They work with lawmakers, advocates, agencies, and organizations who are willing to challenge the status quo and fight to protect our most vulnerable citizens. They are a team of subject matter experts in child protection, policy, and research throughout the United States. They protect children from harm by finding resources, obtaining funding, increasing awareness, advocating for legislative changes, and securing protective measures on social media platforms. I am not a part of RAVEN, but I support what they do.

RESOURCES

- **SHIFT Wellness—Shiftwellness.org**

Supporting Heroes in Mental Health Foundational Training (SHIFT) was developed by The Innocent Justice Foundation (TIJF), a 501(c)(3) nonprofit organization, with funding from the US Department of Justice's Office of Juvenile Justice and Delinquency Prevention (OJJDP). TIJF serves as the training and technical assistance provider for officer wellness, tasked with supporting Internet Crimes Against Children (ICAC) task force teams and affiliated agencies across the United States.

The SHIFT team is comprised of subject matter experts, including globally recognized mental health professionals, ICAC commanders, and frontline professionals, offering a multidisciplinary approach to training and support. SHIFT exists to empower, educate, and support law enforcement and allied professionals through targeted training designed to

- mitigate the negative effects of chronic exposure to child sexual abuse material (CSAM),
- increase individual and team resiliency,
- foster a culture that prioritizes officer wellness.

- **MelKai Consulting—Melkaiconsulting.com**

MelKai Consulting specializes in anti-human trafficking efforts, multidisciplinary team development, and addressing secondary traumatic stress and officer wellness. Over the past decade, MelKai Consulting has provided national and international training and technical assistance to professionals working with victims and survivors of human trafficking.

- **National Center for Missing and Exploited Children (NCMEC)—Missingkids.org**

  NCMEC is the nation's largest and most influential child protection organization. They lead the fight to protect children, creating vital resources for them and the people who keep them safe. NCMEC provides training, case management, clearinghouse resources, analytical support, family and peer support, and recovery services assistance on reports involving child sex trafficking. NCMEC has free online self-paced trainings available. Each of the specialized child sex trafficking trainings was developed in collaboration with compensated lived-experience consultants, alongside child welfare and/or law enforcement professionals, to ensure the resources are informed by the populations they are designed to serve.

- **The International Association of Human Trafficking Investigators (IAHTI)—IAHTI.org**

  IAHTI is a nonprofit organization committed to combatting human trafficking. They empower law enforcement officers, prosecutors, and crime analysts by providing the training, technical and analytical support, resource networks, and secure forums they need to identify victims, dismantle trafficking networks, and hold traffickers accountable. IAHTI consists of active and retired investigators, prosecutors, crime analysts, and survivors of human trafficking—each bringing invaluable, real-world experience to the table. Unlike programs that rely solely on theoretical concepts or textbook knowledge, IAHTI's trainers offer firsthand insights drawn from years of hands-on casework. This unique blend of practical expertise and best practices equips investigators with the tools to identify cases, recover victims, and successfully close human trafficking investigations.

- **RAVEN—Raven.us**

  RAVEN exists to transform our nation's response to child exploitation. As the first and only 501(c)(4) group focused on child exploitation in the United States, they work with lawmakers, advocates, agencies, and organizations who are willing to challenge the status quo and fight to protect our most vulnerable citizens.

- **Forensic Solutions—Forensicsolutions.com**

  Forensic Solutions provides a unique insight into the psychology of sexual offending. Dr. Joe Sullivan and his team provide specialist training on sexual offending, the behavioral analysis behind the crimes, and insight into the minds of perpetrators. This information allows their participants to interpret offender behavior more effectively as well as develop clear, practical skills. The result is that multiagency professionals can improve their practice and inform sensitive decision-making on a daily basis.

ACKNOWLEDGMENTS

Professor Stephen Jaech, I finally finished the book, I hope you like it.

I want to give thanks to Elizabeth Scaife for taking the time to introduce me to so many people that helped and are still helping me do great things. Rebecca Bender, listening to your story changed my perspective when it came to sex trafficking. Thank you for the advice and words of encouragement, and for convincing me to make a TikTok when I absolutely did not want to. Jenna Benton for the words of encouragement when I shared this project with you. Melissa Kaiser for the feedback throughout the creation of this book. Jeremy Lewis and the IAHTI team for welcoming me and providing a platform that allows me to help those still in the fight.

The people that navigated parts of the Ugly with me—John Garden, Brandon Querubin, Ses Maiava, Kyle McNeal, Kristl Pohl, Dan McDonald, William Steen, Anna Gasser, Jake Klein, Anthony Califano, Jennifer Wilcox, Rhonda Tucker, Bryan Ducommon, Randy Drake, Ron Mead, James Mjor, Jason Keays, Tony Doughty, Steve Munson, Gabriel Stajduhar, and Kelly Smith. We helped a lot of people together.

My friends that kept me on track and checked on me along the way—ZSweets, Shooter, Tequila Girl, Doc Jen, Moe, and Fonzo.

Kathleen Healy-Mannfolk, thanks for putting up with me throughout this process. "We like that. We like that."

ABOUT THE AUTHOR

CARLOS RODRIGUEZ is a former crimes-against-children detective sergeant and FBI Task Force Officer (TFO), retiring from the Washington State Patrol (WSP) in June of 2020. Throughout his career, he led teams focused on complex investigations, with his most meaningful work centered on protecting children from sexual abuse and commercial sexual exploitation.

Carlos led WSP's Missing and Exploited Children Task Force (MECTF), which was collocated with the FBI's South Sound Child Exploitation Task Force. He developed proactive investigative operations targeting those who attempt to sexually exploit children, which have been nationally modeled and replicated in jurisdictions across the United States. Carlos is a nationally recognized subject matter expert and continues to present on human trafficking and child exploitation at national and international conferences.

He served as the chief program officer for the International Association of Human Trafficking Investigators (IAHTI), where he helped shape strategy and training initiatives to combat exploitation.

He continues to volunteer for IAHTI, by providing training and guidance as needed.

Currently, Carlos is an internal investigator for the San Diego Unified School District (SDUSD), where he leads investigations involving employee misconduct, student safety, and Title IX violations. He also serves as the point of contact for the district's human trafficking prevention program.

In addition, Carlos volunteers his time to organizations that protect children and vulnerable persons. He is a RAVEN Ambassador (RAVEN.us) and believes in the power of policy to protect children online.

Carlos remains deeply committed to safeguarding children and supporting those on the frontlines of prevention and intervention.

www.ingramcontent.com/pod-product-compliance
Lightning Source LLC
Chambersburg PA
CBHW031536150726
47990CB00001B/190